THE ROUGH GUIDE TO

ST LUCIA

Forthcoming titles include

Chicago • Corfu • First-Time Around the World
Frankfurt Map • Grand Canyon • Los Angeles Map
Philippines • South America • The Gambia
Walks in and around London

Forthcoming reference titles include

The Beatles • Books for Teenagers • Formula 1
Rough Guide Chronicle: Islam • The Universe

read Rough Guides online

www.roughguides.com

Rough Guide Credits

Text editor: Julie Feiner and Caroline Osborne
Series editor: Mark Ellingham
Production: Rachel Holmes
Cartography: Katie Lloyd-Jones
Proofreader: Judith Bamber

Publishing Information

This second edition published January 2003
by Rough Guides Ltd,
80 Strand, London WC2R 0RL

Distributed by the Penguin Group:

Penguin Books Ltd, 80 Strand, London WC2R 0RL.
Penguin Putnam, Inc. 375 Hudson Street, New York 10014, USA
Penguin Books Australia Ltd, 487 Maroondah Highway,
PO Box 257, Ringwood, Victoria 3134, Australia
Penguin Books Canada Ltd, 10 Alcorn Avenue,
Toronto, Ontario, Canada M4V 1E4
Penguin Books (NZ) Ltd,
182–190 Wairau Road, Auckland 10, New Zealand

Typeset in Bembo and Helvetica to an original design by Henry Iles.
Printed in Spain by Graphy Cems.

© Karl Luntta 2003
272pp, includes index
A catalogue record for this book is available from the British Library.

ISBN 1-85828-916-5

THE **ROUGH GUIDE** TO

ST LUCIA

by Karl Luntta

This edition researched and updated by Nicky Agate

ROUGH
GUIDES

We set out to do something different when the first Rough Guide was published in 1982. Mark Ellingham, just out of university, was travelling in Greece. He brought along the popular guides of the day, but found they were all lacking in some way. They were either strong on ruins and museums but went on for pages without mentioning a beach or taverna. Or they were so conscious of the need to save money that they lost sight of Greece's cultural and historical significance. Also, none of the books told him anything about Greece's contemporary life – its politics, its culture, its people, and how they lived.

So with no job in prospect, Mark decided to write his own guidebook, one which aimed to provide practical information that was second to none, detailing the best beaches and the hottest clubs and restaurants, while also giving hard-hitting accounts of every sight, both famous and obscure, and providing up-to-the-minute information on contemporary culture. It was a guide that encouraged independent travellers to find the best of Greece, and was a great success, getting shortlisted for the Thomas Cook travel guide award, and encouraging Mark, along with three friends, to expand the series.

The Rough Guide list grew rapidly and the letters flooded in, indicating a much broader readership than had been anticipated, but one which uniformly appreciated the Rough Guide mix of practical detail and humour, irreverence and enthusiasm. Things haven't changed. The same four friends who began the series are still the caretakers of the Rough Guide mission today: to provide the most reliable, up-to-date and entertaining information to independent-minded travellers of all ages, on all budgets.

We now publish more than 300 titles and have offices in London and New York. The travel guides are written and researched by a dedicated team of more than 200 authors, based in Britain, Europe, the USA and Australia. We have also created a unique series of phrasebooks to accompany the travel series, along with an acclaimed series of music guides, and a best-selling pocket guide to the Internet and World Wide Web. We also publish comprehensive travel information on our website: **www.roughguides.com**

Help us update

We've gone to a lot of trouble to ensure that this Rough Guide is as up to date and accurate as possible. However, things do change. All suggestions, comments and corrections are much appreciated, and we'll send a copy of the next edition (or any other Rough Guide if you prefer) for the best letters.

Please mark letters **"Rough Guide St Lucia Update"** and send to:

Rough Guides, 80 Strand, London WC2R 0RL or
Rough Guides, 4th Floor, 345 Hudson St, New York NY 10014.

Or send an email to mail@roughguides.com
Have your questions answered and tell others about your trip at
www.roughguides.atinfopop.com

Acknowledgements

Karl Luntta would like to thank Wenda and all at the St Lucia Tourist Board offices in Castries and Soufrière, and Marcella Martinez, Laura Davidson and Marilyn Marx.

Nicky Agate would like to thank Tanya Warner at the St Lucia Tourist Board, Andrew Davies at Capri, Verena Lawaetz at St Lucia Heritage Tours, Peter Lang at Budget and everyone at Rough Guides in New York, particularly the ever-patient Julie Feiner and the ever-absent Richard Koss. She also sends out love to Nick and Jenny Agate for their support, Kate McConnell and Damaris Cozza for their phone line, and Richard Nisa for ensuring that the cruise ships didn't win.

Readers' letters

John Black, Pat Clark, Carrie Drake, Barbara Elias, Rien Huiskamp, Edward Pardoe, Ed Potter, Robert Price, Janie Roserie, Fleur Simper, Stephen Thorpe, Peter Waghorn, Rachel Wright.

Cover credits

Main front picture ©Robert Harding
Small front picture Heliconia caribaea ©Getty
Back top picture Petit Piton ©John Miller
Back lower picture Soufrière ©Imagestate

CONTENTS

The Guide 53

Listings 149

Contexts 223

MAP LIST

MAP SYMBOLS

═══	Road	★	Bus stop
───	Waterway	P	Parking
♦	Point of interest	✚	Hospital
⌂	Mountain range	⊠	Post office
▲	Mountain peak	ⓘ	Information office
⚱	Waterfall	⛵	Windsurfing
⋀⋀	Spring	▬	Building
∴	Ruins	✚	Church
⬡	Turtle nesting site	⊞	Cemetery
⚘	Gardens	▨	Park or reserve
◉	Restaurant or bar	⌇	Mangrove swamp
✈	Airport	⣿	Beach

Introduction

St Lucia more than lives up to the paradisal Caribbean stereotype: a glorious mix of honey-sand beaches, translucent waters sheltering reefs swarming with tropical fish, lush interior rainforests and a thriving culture that encompasses literature and theatre as well as music and dance. However, in contrast to other islands in the region, where the tourism infrastructure has been steadily expanding since the 1960s, St Lucia has only recently begun to attract visitors in any number. As a result, tourism has a much lower profile here, and this low-key feel is one of the island's biggest assets. With little of the jaded hustle that can mar more established Caribbean destinations, you'll find St Lucia a relaxed, informal and incredibly friendly place to visit, especially if you venture out of the heavily touristed enclaves in and around Rodney Bay and take the time to explore Marigot Bay, Soufrière and – even more authentic – the small villages of the Atlantic coast and the south. Here, you'll find plenty of inexpensive, no-frills guesthouses, roadside dining establishments and open-air village markets. If you'd rather take advantage of the more established tourist facilities, be aware that those that do exist are typically top-notch and predominantly designed for the rather well-to-do, with luxury hotels, world-class restaurants and large duty-free malls to indulge in the odd shopping spree.

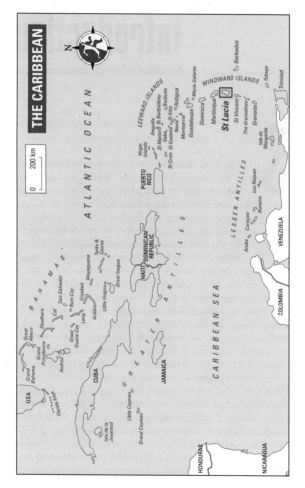

It's probably best to shoot for a range of experiences, and there's really no reason not to: St Lucia's 616 square kilometres are ripe for exploration, and though a rental car is the optimum way to get around, bus links to most areas are good and taxis are always available. If it is **beaches** you're after, you'll probably head first to the tourism strongholds of the **northwest coast**, where scores of hotels and restaurants are clustered in **Rodney Bay** and on the stretch between that village and **Gros Islet**. Reef-fringed swaths of white sand along this stretch of coastline justify its "Golden Mile" nickname. There's plenty of historical intrigue – as well as more idyllic seashores – at former pirate hangout and British military bastion **Pigeon Island**, on a spit of land just northwest of the tourist enclaves; the remains of stone **forts** scattered throughout the area are a telling reminder of the fierce Anglo-French battles for possession of St Lucia, which saw the "Helen of the West Indies" change hands more than a dozen times. South of Rodney Bay, the bustling capital of **Castries** is also worth visiting, with its grassy town square named after St Lucia's Nobel Prize-winning author Derek Walcott, and a clamorous, colourful market that provides vivid insight into everyday island life. Castries is also surrounded by some decaying fortifications, such as Fort Charlotte and La Toc Battery; the odd wondrous beach is also within easy reach of the city.

These days, visitors are gravitating more and more to the **south** of the island, where the pace is slower and the bays are lined with brightly painted fishing boats rather than the garish concrete of resort hotels. With a deep-water harbour framed by St Lucia's best-known landmark – the monolithic twin peaks of the **Pitons** – the attractive, laid-back town of **Soufrière** boasts gorgeous colonial architecture as well as unusual stretches of dark grey-brown volcanic sand. Within reach of the town are numerous attractions: sugarcane **plantations** established by French and English colonists

ELEVEN THINGS NOT TO MISS

Central Market, Castries All manner of excellent produce, worthy crafts and tacky souvenirs are on display at this bustling hangout; the restaurant stalls are the prime place in town for a cheap, delicious meal. See p.64

"Jump-up" on Friday night This booze-and-music fuelled celebration is St Lucia's weekly street party, when crowds gather on Gros Islet to eat, dance and drink and be merry. See p.87

Cas En Bas beaches Reduit Beach, not far away, is spectacular but crowded; head further on to these usually deserted spots to claim your own patch of sand. See p.88

Anse La Raye's fish fry A tiny fishing village between Castries and Soufrière, Anse La Raye is quiet until Friday evenings, when everyone flocks to the streets to sample that day's freshest fish, barbecued and served alongside helpings of hot cakes and booze. See p.102

La Soufrière Sulphur Springs Visit St Lucia's most famous attraction, La Soufrière Sulphur Springs – a great, odiferous bubbling crater. See p.110

Balenbouche Estate Maybe not the grandest of St Lucia's plantation houses, but the one here does function as a very atmospheric guesthouse; wandering round the extensive

have been opened up to the public or transformed into **botanical gardens**, while the bubbling, malodorous **La Soufrière Sulphur Springs** have been re-packaged as the world's only "drive-in" volcano. These mineral-rich waters have been harnessed at nearby **Diamond Estate**, where you can take a restorative bath in an outdoor pool.

Southern St Lucia is also the most convenient starting point for excursions into the rainforest-smothered mountains of the **interior forest reserves**. Laced with **hiking trails**, abundant with swimmable **waterfalls** and home to

grounds opens up access to petroglyph sites and a nearby secluded beach. See p.118

Mamiku Gardens Admire the elegance of these perfectly manicured botanical gardens along any of its low-impact walking trails. See p.129

Frigate birds and leatherback turtles Be one of the few visitors to explore the much wilder Atlantic Coast, where the Fregate Island Nature Reserve and Grand Anse hold great wildlife-spotting opportunities. See pp.131 & 134

Hiking in the rainforest Choose from one of five forestry department trails, which vary from a forty-minute stroll to a half-day trek, through the thickets of St Lucia's rainforest reserves. See p.138

Foxgrove Inn, Praslin Bay *Foxgrove Inn* on the eastern side of the island has one of the best locally regarded restaurants, serving super fresh fish and seafood on a balcony overlooking banana plantations and the wild surf around the Fregate Islands. See p.195

Snorkeling around the Pitons Rather than hiking for the fine views, go underwater near the mountains' bases, to find reefs, rocks and impossibly coloured fish. See p.209

some rare and exotic **wildlife**, the forests provide an absorbing alternative to beach life; perhaps the most accessible of these, if you're staying in the south, is the **Des Cartiers Rainforest**, inland from the east coast highway.

While you're out this way, see more of St Lucia's tropical environment at the protected **nature reserves** along the southeast coast: the Fregate and Maria islands are home to magnificent frigate birds and endemic lizards, while pristine offshore reefs make for great snorkelling. Windswept, wild and pounded by the Atlantic Ocean, the spectacular beaches of the east coast are better for hiking than for swimming, and **leatherback turtles** visit more regularly than tourists.

A fusion of French, British and African traditions, St Lucia's Creole **culture** is an intriguing mix: while the official language is English, the lingua franca is a mellifluous, French-based Patois that employs African vocabulary and structures. Similarly, the local **cuisine** blends French traditions with island ingredients, focusing on local seafood and root crops originally imported from Africa on slave ships. However, the most conspicuous – and exciting – expressions of St Lucia's culture are its **festivals**, Christian in origin but African in character. **Carnival** is by far the biggest event, a colourful, animated round of frenetic parties, calypso contests and parades of revellers decked out in wild costumes portraying spirits and devils – probably most exuberantly celebrated in the Castries area. If you're not lucky enough to be in St Lucia for Carnival, or for the more intimate summer saints' festivals, you haven't entirely missed out. The St Lucian propensity for partying is indulged each Friday when the tiny village of Gros Islet is overtaken by a classic West Indian **"jump-up"**, a street party where tourists and locals alike descend for a night of eating, drinking and dancing under the stars. St Lucia's fastest-growing event, the annual **Jazz Festival** is a more sophisticated gathering, with some of the genre's biggest names performing under the palm trees of Pigeon Island, as well as in grassy spaces down in Vieux Fort, in the south.

When to go

For many visitors, St Lucia's biggest attraction is its tropical **climate**. During the mid-December to mid-April high season, the island is pleasantly hot, with little rain and constant northeasterly trade winds keeping the nights cool. Temperatures rise during the summer months, which can also be wet: the rainy season lasts from June to October, and during this time, short, heavy bursts of rain are matched by an increase in humidity; rainfall is nearly three times heavier in the central rainforests than along the coast. The rainy months also coincide with the **hurricane season**, which runs roughly from late August to October.

As you'd expect, St Lucia is busiest in the first few months of the year; during this time, some beaches, particularly those in the northwest, are likely to be crowded, and hotel prices are at their peak. The rest of the year, accommodation rates, airfares and even car rental prices can decrease significantly.

St Lucia's climate

	F°		C°		RAINFALL	
	AVERAGE DAILY		AVERAGE DAILY		AVERAGE MONTHLY	
	MAX	MIN	MAX	MIN	IN	MM
Jan	82	69	28	21	5.3	135
Feb	83	69	28	21	3.6	91
March	84	69	29	21	3.8	97
April	87	71	31	22	3.4	96
May	88	73	31	23	5.9	150
June	88	74	31	23	8.6	218
July	87	74	31	23	9.3	236
Aug	88	74	31	23	10.6	269
Sept	88	73	31	23	9.9	252
Oct	87	72	31	22	9.3	236
Nov	85	71	29	22	9.1	231
Dec	83	70	28	21	7.8	798

BASICS

Getting there

By far the easiest and cheapest way to get to St Lucia is by air. Indeed, unless you travel here on one of the many cruise ships, which typically dock here for less than a day, or are coming from a nearby Caribbean island, which has a ferry service to and from St Lucia (see p.19), an international flight is just about your only option. Regardless of where you buy your ticket, fares will depend on the season. These vary from airline to airline, but mid-December to mid-April is generally classified as high season, with low season more or less the rest of the year, except if you're travelling from the UK, from where July and August see a return to high season fares.

You can normally cut costs by going through a consolidator or discount agent, who may offer **student and youth fares** and a range of other services such as travel insurance, car rental and tours. Penalties for changing your plans, however, can be stiff. Some agencies specialize in **charter flights**, which may be cheaper than anything available on a scheduled flight, but the disadvantage with these is that they usually have set departure and return dates, limiting flexibility by only offering holidays in seven-day blocks, and of one- to three-weeks' duration. It's also worth bearing in mind that charter airlines have been known to cancel flights that aren't filled, sometimes with less than satisfactory reimbursement to ticket holders, and that schedules may change without warning.

A further possibility for finding a deal on airfare is the **internet**, where many airlines and discount-travel websites offer you the opportunity to book your tickets online at often drastically reduced rates; besides the airlines' individual sites, check out: ⓦ www.travelocity.com, ⓦ www.expedia .com, ⓦ www.cheapflights.com and ⓦ www.hotwire.com.

International flights arrive at **Hewanorra International Airport** in Vieux Fort; **George F.L. Charles Airport** in Castries services regional flights for the Caribbean; see pp.58 and 115 for arrival information.

Package trips to St Lucia can be very good value, often costing less than the sum of flights and accommodation bought separately, and sometimes including extras such as a rental car. Specialist trips are also available, focusing on activities such as scuba diving. You'll often have to stay for at least three nights (sometimes seven) and take a set number of meals in the hotel, but the savings can be significant. When booking packages, however, remember that most rates are quoted per person based upon two people sharing a room. The fare for a single traveller is often more than half of that for two. If you're looking to get married in St Lucia, Awesome Caribbean Weddings (☏ 758/540 0300, ⓦ www.awesomecaribbeanweddings.com) is a wedding and honeymoon package company based on the island that will arrange everything except your flight.

For more information on St Lucia weddings, see Chapter 11, Directory.

GETTING THERE

Lastly, if you plan to indulge in some **island hopping** around the Caribbean from St Lucia, BWIA or LIAT air passes can be worthwhile (see p.17).

FROM BRITAIN AND IRELAND

The great majority of British and Irish visitors to St Lucia arrive on a **direct charter flight** as part of a package holiday – and even if you plan to travel independently this is still the cheapest way to get here.

When it comes to direct **scheduled flights**, the choice is limited: Virgin fly once a week direct from London Gatwick and once via Antigua; BWIA (British West Indian Airline) depart twice weekly from London Heathrow; and BA have three flights a week via Antigua.

FARES AND FLIGHTS

The **cost** of flights from Britain and Ireland to St Lucia varies widely, depending on the time of year. High season is July and August and Christmas/New Year's, low season from April to July and September. October to November and January to March are considered the shoulder season.

As well as agents and consolidators, check travel ads in the weekend papers, the holiday pages of ITV's Teletext and, in London, *Time Out* and the *Evening Standard*. Free magazines aimed at young travellers, such as *TNT*, are also useful resources. Your cheapest **charter option** is likely to be Air 2000, which flies once a week on Sundays from London Gatwick.

Virgin has a direct **scheduled flight** from London Gatwick on Sunday, and also flies nonstop five times a week to Barbados (not Wed or Sun) and Antigua (Wed), with a connecting flight on local airline LIAT to St Lucia. BWIA

GETTING THERE

has a twice-weekly service (Tues & Sun) from Heathrow. British Airways also fly three times a week from London Gatwick (Tues, Thurs & Sun), touching down in Antigua. Fares average around £525 during the low season and rise to as much as £850 at the height of the high season.

Flights from **regional airports** in the UK all go via London Gatwick: BA fly from Manchester and Glasgow via Gatwick to St Lucia; while from Belfast there are British European, British Midland and Lufthansa flights to Gatwick, connecting on to St Lucia with BA. From Dublin BA flies to St Lucia via Gatwick as well.

Airlines

Air 2000 ℡ 0870/757 2 757, ⓦ www.air2000.com.

British Airways ℡ 0845/773 3377, in Ireland ℡ 1800/626 747, ⓦ www.britishairways.com.

British European ℡ 0870/5676 676, in Ireland ℡ 890/925 532, ⓦ www.flybe.com.

British Midland ℡ 1-800/788-0555, ⓦ www.flybmi.com.

BWIA ℡ 0208/577 1100, in Ireland ℡ 01/201 3915 ⓦ www.bwee.com.

Lufthansa ℡ 0845/7737 747, ⓦ www.luthansa.co.uk.

Virgin Atlantic ℡ 01293/450 150, ⓦ www.virgin-atlantic.com.

Discount travel agents

Bridge the World 45–47 Chalk Farm Rd, London NW1 8AJ ℡ 0870/444 7474, ⓦ www.bridgetheworld.com.

Campus Travel 52 Grosvenor Gardens, London SW1W 0AG and all over the UK ℡ 0870/240 1010, ⓦ www.campustravel.co.uk.

Cheap Flights ⓦ www.cheapflights.co.uk.

Flightbookers 177 Tottenham Court Rd, London W1P 0LX plus a branch at Gatwick airport ℡ 0870/010 7000, ⓦ www.ebookers.com/uk.

Joe Walsh Tours 8 Lower Baggot St, Dublin 2, ℡ 01/676 3053, ⓦ www.joewalshtours.ie;

other branches in Dublin and in Cork.

The London Flight Centre 125 Earls Court Rd, London SW5 9RH ⊤ 020/7244 6411, ⓦ www.topdecktravel.co.uk/flights.htm; plus other branches in London.

North South Travel Moulsham Mill Centre, Parkway, Chelmsford, Essex CM2 7PX ⊤ 01245/608 291, ⓦ www.northsouthtravel.co.uk.

STA Travel 40 Bernard St, London WC1N 1LJ plus branches all over London and the UK ⊤ 08701/600 599; Northern Ireland 92–94 Botanic Ave, Belfast BT7 1JR ⊤ 02890/241 469, ⓦ www.statravel.co.uk.

Trailfinders 1 Threadneedle St, London EC2R 8JX ⊤ 020/7628 7628, ⓦ www.trailfinders.co.uk; 4–5 Dawson St, Dublin 2 ⊤ 01/677 7888; plus branches in Belfast, Birmingham, Bristol, Glasgow and Manchester.

USIT Now Fountain Centre, College St, Belfast BT1 6ET ⊤ 02890/327 111, ⓦ www.usitnow.com; 19–21 Aston Quay, O'Connell Bridge, Dublin 2 ⊤ 01/602 1600; plus various other locations in Ireland ⓦ www.usitnow.ie.

PACKAGES AND TOURS

There is a wealth of **package tour** operators to choose from with accommodation ranging from self-catering apartments to full-on luxury hotels: a selection is given on p.8. Virgin Holidays offer amongst the cheapest deals: they have an all-inclusive week-long vacation starting at £869, including transfers. Thomas Cook offers similar all-inclusive packages, with special deals available for honeymooners and repeat visitors. In Ireland, Joe Walsh has departures from Dublin, Cork and Shannon, with onward British Airways/BWIA connections via Heathrow; prices start at around €2284 per week, all-inclusive.

GETTING THERE

Specialist package and tour operators

Caribbean Holidays 4 Less
Ⓣ 020/7400 7017, Ⓦ www
.caribbean-holidays4less
.co.uk.

Complete Caribbean
Ⓣ 01423/531 031, Ⓦ www
.completecaribbean.co.uk.

Hayes & Jarvis Ⓣ 0870/898
9890, Ⓦ www.hayesandjarvis
.co.uk.

Joe Walsh Tours Ⓣ 01/676
3053, Ⓦ www.joewalshtours.ie

Kuoni Ⓣ 01306/747 002,
Ⓦ www.kuoni.co.uk.

Suntext Ⓣ 01892/616 000,
Ⓦ www.suntext.com

Thomas Cook Ⓣ 0870/0100
437, Ⓦ www.thomascook
.co.uk.

Tropical Places Ⓣ 0870/160
5015, Ⓦ www.tropicalplaces
.co.uk.

Virgin Holidays Ⓣ 0870/220
2788, Ⓦ www.virginholidays
.co.uk.

FROM THE USA AND CANADA

In testament to the island's popularity as a holiday destination for North Americans, flights are on a daily basis during the high season, with services only slightly reduced in the low season. Air Canada fly once a week from Toronto and US Airways has a weekly direct flight from Philadelphia to St Lucia; from New York JFK, Air Jamaica go via Grenada or Antigua, BWIA via Port of Spain and American Airlines via San Juan and all have domestic connections; JetBlue and United also fly to San Juan from JFK and Continental flies there from Washington – it's easy to pick up an American Eagle connecting flight from San Juan to St Lucia. BWIA also fly from Miami.

FARES AND FLIGHTS

Typical **scheduled return fares** from New York JFK range from US$450 to US$790, depending on the season, with

December to April seeing the highest fares. That said, there are often great deals to be had from the US during the busy high season, with prices closer to the low end of the range. Air Canada operates the only direct flight from Canada, a once-weekly affair from Toronto to Hewanorra on Saturdays – fares are about CAN$1100–$1200 year round.

With four months advance purchase, vigilant web fare watching and special offers from airlines, these fares can be substantially reduced. It's also worth bearing in mind that you may pay as much as US$80 more if you choose to fly to George F.L. Charles Airport in Castries rather than the main international airport, Hewanorra, in the south of the island – but if you are staying at any of the resorts near Rodney Bay, you'll save that again on taxi fares and transfers.

One of the more frequent and reliable **charter companies** is GWV International, which offers three-, four- and seven-night charter/package deals (you must stay at a designated hotel) during the high season. However, you cannot contact GWV directly (though the website listed below gives schedules), and all of their flights and packages must be booked through travel agents.

Airlines

Air Canada in US ☏ 1800/776 3000, in Canada 800/268 7240, Ⓦ www.aircanada.ca. Direct flights to St Lucia on Saturdays from Toronto.

Air Jamaica ☏ 1800/523 5585, Ⓦ www.airjamaica.com. Several flights a week (daily in high season) from New York to Hewanorra via Grenada and Antigua, plus services via Jamaica from Atlanta, Baltimore, Chicago, Houston, Philadelphia, Los Angeles, Fort Lauderdale, Miami and Newark.

American Airlines ☏ 1800/433 7300, Ⓦ www.aa.com. Daily flights to Hewanorra from major cities via Miami and New York. From San Juan in Puerto Rico, AA's

subsidiary **American Eagle**
ⓣ 1-800/433-7300 connects
several times daily to George
F.L. Charles Airport.

BWIA ⓣ 1888/853 8560,
ⓦ www.bwee.com.
Several flights per week from
Miami and New York, via
Antigua and Port of Spain.

Continental Airlines
ⓣ 1800/231-0856,
ⓦ www.continental.com.
Flights from Washington to
San Juan, where connections
to St Lucia can be made with
American Eagle (see above).

GWV No phone, ⓦ www
.gwvtravel.com. Charter
company offering
charter/package deals.

JetBlue ⓣ 1800/538 2583,
ⓦ www.jetblue.com. Daily
flights from JFK to San Juan,
where connections to St Lucia
can be made with American
Eagle (see above).

Sunquest Vacations
ⓣ 1877/485 6060, ⓦ www
.sunquest.ca. Toronto-based
charter airline with occasional
flights to St Lucia; schedules
change regularly.

United Airlines ⓣ 1800/538-
2929, ⓦ www.ual.com. Daily
flights from JFK to San Juan,
where connections to St Lucia
can be made with American
Eagle (see opposite).

US Airways ⓣ 1800/428 4322,
ⓦ www.usairways.com.
Saturday flights only from
Philadelphia to St Lucia.

Discount travel agents and consolidators

Air Courier Association
ⓣ 1800/282 1202,
ⓦ www.aircourier.org.

STA Travel ⓣ 1 800/781 4040,
ⓦ www.sta-travel.com;
branches in New York, Tempe,
Tucson, Los Angeles, San
Francisco, Washington DC,
Orlando, Atlanta, Chicago,
New Orleans, Boston,
Minneapolis, Las Vegas,
Philadelphia, Austin, Seattle
and many other college towns
in the US.

Travel Avenue ⓣ 1800/333
3335, ⓦ www.travelavenue
.com.

Travel CUTS ⓣ 1866/246 9762,
ⓦ www.travelcuts.com;
branches all over Canada.

PACKAGES

- -

Package trips can be arranged through any of the tour operators listed below; the agents listed opposite should be able to search out a deal that suits your budget and any special interests too. It's also worth scanning the Sunday travel sections of large city newspapers for special deals. Package prices can vary considerably, depending on the class of your accommodation (all-inclusives, for example, will obviously cost more), but two people sharing a room can expect to pay from US$1500 to $2350 per person for flights and a week's accommodation during the high season, and from US$1000 to $1500 per person in the low season.

Tour operators

Air Jamaica Vacations No phone, ⓦ www.airjamaica vacations.com.

American Airlines Vacations ⓣ 1800/321 2121,

ⓦ www.aavacations.com.

Empress Travel and Cruises ⓣ 1800/246 6620,
ⓦ www.empressonline.com.

Liberty Travel ⓣ 212/580-7100,
ⓦ www.libertytravel.com.

CRUISES

- -

Cruises are a popular way to visit – albeit briefly – a number of Caribbean destinations, including St Lucia, with trips lasting three days, six to nine days or ten or more days. The average length of stay in a port is a day or less. Rates are based on "inside" or "outside" cabins (with or without ocean view, respectively), for one or two persons per cabin. Most Caribbean cruises depart from Miami, Fort Lauderdale or Tampa, or San Juan, Puerto Rico.

The cruise lines listed overleaf are among the most popular with St Lucia as a destination. Typical rates given are for an inside cabin in high season, excluding port fees (US$120–165) and any airfare.

Cruise lines

Carnival Cruise Lines
Ⓣ 1-800/327-9501, Ⓦ www
.carnival.com. US$799 (7
days).

Celebrity Cruise Lines
Ⓣ 1-800/437-3111,
Ⓦ www.celebritycruises.com.

US$1939 (7 days); US$4259
(10 days).

Holland America Line
Ⓣ 1-877/932-4589,
Ⓦ www.hollandamerica.com.
US$1420 (10 days).

Princess Cruises Ⓣ 1-800/421-
0522, Ⓦ www.princess.com.
US$1119 (7 days).

FROM AUSTRALIA AND NEW ZEALAND

The Caribbean is not a bargain destination from **Australia**
or **New Zealand**. With no direct flights to St Lucia, the
only way to get there is to take a flight to one of the main
gateway US airports, and pick up onward connections from
there.

Generally, the least expensive and most straightforward
routes are via New York or Miami. Both are served by regular flights to George F.L. Charles Airport in Castries and
to Hewanorra airport in Vieux Fort. If you're planning to
see St Lucia as part of a longer trip, **round-the-world**
(RTW) tickets are worth considering, as they're usually better value than a simple return flight. Whatever kind of ticket you're after, your first move should be to call one of the
specialist agents listed on p.14.

FARES, FLIGHTS AND RTW TICKETS

From **Australia**, the most direct **routes** you're likely to
find are the Air New Zealand, United and Qantas regular
services to Los Angeles, with connecting flights to New
York or Miami with American Airlines or United, from
where you connect to St Lucia flights. Return **fares** to

New York or Miami from the eastern states of **Australia** on any of these airlines (excluding taxes) cost from A$2390 in the low and shoulder seasons and A$3500 in December and January. If you're not in a hurry, you could also fly with overnight stops on Japan Airlines or South African Airways, for less money. Onward flights from New York and Miami to St Lucia are available with BWIA. (See p.8 for more on connections from North America.)

From New Zealand, Air New Zealand, United and Qantas fly to Los Angeles with connections on to Miami or New York; through-fares to Miami start at NZ$2800 in the low season and NZ$3800 in the high season, both exclusive of taxes. Flights to St Lucia from Auckland (via the US) cost from NZ$3800.

Given these fares and routings, **round-the-world tickets** that take in one of the gateway airports in the United States are worth considering, especially if you have the time to make the most of a few stopovers. Ultimately, your choice of route will depend on where else you want to visit besides St Lucia. Various airlines offer routings including stops in New York or Miami from A$1999/NZ$2699. Call any of the agents or airlines listed for more information.

Airlines

Air New Zealand Australia ⊤ 13/2476; New Zealand ⊤ 0800/737 000, Ⓦ www.airnz.co.nz.

American Airlines Australia ⊤ 1300/650 747, Ⓦ www.aa.com.

BWIA Australia ⊤ 02/9285 6811, New Zealand ⊤ 09/309 8094, Ⓦ www.bwee.com.

Japan Airlines Australia ⊤ 02/9272 1111, New Zealand ⊤ 09/379 9906, Ⓦ www.jal.com.

Qantas Australia ⊤ 13 13 13, New Zealand ⊤ 09/357 8900 or 0800/808 767, Ⓦ www.qantas.com.au.

South African Airways Australia ⊤ 02/9223 4402 or ⊤ 1800/670 150, Ⓦ www.saairways.com.au, New

GETTING THERE

Zealand ℡ 09/309 9132 or
0800/442 707.
United Airlines Australia ℡ 13
1777, ⓦ www.unitedairlines
.com.au; New Zealand
℡ 09/379 3800,
ⓦ www.unitedairlines.co.nz.

Travel agents

Anywhere Travel 345 Anzac
Parade, Kingsford, Sydney
℡ 02/9663 0411.
Budget Travel 16 Fort St,
Auckland ℡ 09/366 0061 or
0800/808040,
ⓦ www.budgettravel.co.nz.
Destinations Unlimited 3
Milford Rd, Milford, Auckland
℡ 09/414 1685,
ⓦ www.holiday.co.nz.
Flight Centres Australia: Level
11, 33 Berry St, North Sydney
℡ 13 3133 (24hr), plus
branches nationwide.
New Zealand: National Bank

Towers, 205–225 Queen St,
Auckland ℡ 0800/354 448,
plus branches nationwide.
ⓦ www.flightcentre.com.
STA Travel Australia: 855
George St, Sydney ℡ 1300
733 035, ⓦ www.statravel.com
.au; branches in most major
cities and college towns. New
Zealand: Shop 2b, 182 Queen
St, Auckland ℡ 0800/874 773,
plus branches in Wellington,
Christchurch, Dunedin, and
most major college towns.
ⓦ www.statravel.co.nz.
Trailfinders 8 Spring St, Sydney
℡ 02/9247 7666 with
branches in Perth, Melbourne,
Cairns and Brisbane.
ⓦ www.trailfinders.com.au.
Travel.com 80 Clarence St,
Sydney ℡ 02/9290 1500 or
1300/430 482, ⓦ www.travel
.com.au.

PACKAGES AND CRUISES

Package holidays to St Lucia from Australia and New
Zealand are few and far between, and many specialists act as
agents for US-based operators, simply adding a return flight
from Australia onto the cost. **Cruises** account for a large
sector of the market: most depart from Miami or Fort
Lauderdale, and because prices are based on US dollar
amounts, they fluctuate with the exchange rate. To give

some idea, all-inclusive eleven-day cruises calling at seven islands including St Lucia start at A$880 (A$2870 including airfare from Australia). The luxury end of the market is catered for by Caribbean Destinations and Contours, both of which offer resort- and villa-based holidays as well as cruises, with a choice of accommodation in St Lucia – mostly in self-contained resort complexes. Prices start at around A$4000 for fourteen days, based on low-season air-fares from Australia and two people sharing a room.

Specialist agents and tour operators

Caribbean Destinations Level 1, North Tower, The Rialto, 525 Collins St, Melbourne ⓣ1800/354 104, ⓦwww.caribbeanislands.com.au.

Contours 466 Victoria St, North Melbourne ⓣ03/9670 6900, ⓔcountourstravel@bigpond.com.au.

Mediterranean Shipping Cruises Level 8, 155 George St, Sydney ⓣ1800/028 502, ⓦwww.msc.com.au.

Wiltrans Level 10, 189 Kent St, Sydney ⓣ02/9255 0899.

GETTING THERE

Caribbean island hopping

t's not difficult to use St Lucia as a launch pad for visits to other Caribbean islands. Flying is naturally the fastest way to do it, and several pan-Caribbean airlines ply routes between the islands, with daily services (not necessarily nonstop) to and from St Lucia. Make sure you carry your passport or identification when you fly, and an outward ticket for departing St Lucia. Ferry services between some Eastern Caribbean islands are also worth considering; they take a little longer, but are less expensive than flying. To organize your island hopping, call the airlines directly before you leave or when in St Lucia – numbers are listed on p.18; once there, you can also call in at one of the local travel agents listed on p.220.

FLIGHTS

George F.L. Charles Airport in Castries is the hub for inter-island travel, and it's here that you'll find ticket counters for the American Airlines subsidiary **American Eagle**, which flies daily to San Juan with onward connections to major

North American cities. American Eagle make connections from St Lucia to most Caribbean islands via its San Juan hub; main destinations include St Thomas, St Croix, St Maarten, Anguilla, the Dominican Republic, Aruba, Grenada and St Kitts; round-trip fares average at just below the EC$1000 mark. **British West Indies Airways (BWIA)** connects St Lucia to Trinidad and Tobago, Antigua, Barbados, Jamaica, Grenada, St Martin, Caracas and Guyana, as well as New York and Miami; again, round-trip fares average at around EC$1000. Based in Antigua, **Leeward Islands Air Transport (LIAT)** is one of the Caribbean's busiest carriers, though not always the most efficient, flying to nearly every island in the Eastern Caribbean, and nonstop from St Lucia to Antigua, Barbados, Martinique, Trinidad and St Vincent. Return fares range from EC$296 to nearby St Vincent, to EC$748 to St Thomas in the US Virgin Islands. **Air Martinique** services St Martin and Martinique. From St Lucia, sample return fares (exclusive of taxes) include EC$282 to Martinique on Air Martinique, and EC$389 to Barbados on LIAT.

AIR PASSES

If you're planning to visit more than a couple of islands, it's worth considering a **multi-destination ticket**, such as those offered by **LIAT**. Their Caribbean Super Explorer costs US$575 plus applicable departure taxes (averaging US$10) and allows unlimited travel for thirty days to any LIAT destination (one stopover per destination). The scaled-back Explorer fare allows three stopovers within twenty days with return to your point of origin for US$300 plus taxes. Discounts are offered for senior citizens and children and European travellers can also avail themselves of Caribbean air passes, sold at US$98 a sector. Between three and six sector passes must be bought at the same time, and all of these passes must be purchased simultaneously with your ticket – on any airline – to the Caribbean (contact LIAT through your travel agent at home). Bear in mind, however, that schedules can be unreliable so it's important to reconfirm all flights. Trinidad-based **BWIA** offer similar **island-hopper fares** from time to time. Currently, these cost US\$399 in economy and US\$599 in first class and allow travel between BWIA's twelve Caribbean destinations in a thirty day period. Availability can be somewhat sporadic, so call for current information once in St Lucia (☎452–3778 or 452–3789). Air Jamaica also offer a Caribbean Hopper Program, which enables a US-originating passenger to visit three or more islands for US\$399 for economy class and US\$699 for first class for travel within their Caribbean and Central American network. Contact Air Jamaica in the US on ☎1800/523 5585 for more information.

Airlines

Air Jamaica in UK ☎020 8570 9171; in US ☎1-800/523-5585; in St Lucia ☎453-6611.
Air Martinique ☎452-2463 or 453-6660.
American Airlines In UK ☎0845/789789, in US ☎1-800/433-7300, in St Lucia ☎454-6777.
American Eagle in St Lucia ☎452-1820.
British West Indies Airlines (BWIA) in UK ☎020/8577 1120, in US ☎1-800/327-7401, in St Lucia ☎452/3778.
Leeward Islands Air Transport (LIAT) in St Lucia ☎452-2348 or 452-3056.

FERRIES

St Lucia's closest neighbours are easily accessible by **sea**. The **L'Express des Iles** high-speed passenger ferry currently leaves Castries for Guadeloupe three times per week (Wed 1pm, Sun 1pm, Sat 7am; 1hr 20min); the Wednesday and Saturday sailings stop in Martinique, and both these and the Sunday trip stop at Dominica as well. Additional sailings for Martinique leave three times a week (Mon 7am, Tues 5pm, Fri 1pm) In addition to a departure tax of EC$20, you'll pay EC$275 for a round-trip ticket, which allows a stop in Martinique or Dominica at no extra cost. A ten percent discount is available to those under 26 or over 60. The ferry is represented by Cox and Company in Castries – for information and latest schedules, call ☎ 452-2211 or see ⓦ www.express-des-iles.com.

Visas and red tape

Citizens of Britain, the US and Canada can enter St Lucia without a visa and stay for up to 42 days; longer stays must be arranged through the St Lucia immigration department (☎ 454-6239) once on the island. You'll need to produce either a passport or photo identification such as a driver's licence plus proof of citizenship (birth certificate, residency card, etc). On production of a passport, citizens of Australia, New Zealand and all other

Commonwealth countries and Ireland can enter without a visa and stay for up to 28 days, after which you have to apply to the St Lucia immigration department. Generally speaking, it's wise for citizens of all countries to travel with a passport.

All visitors are required to show a ticket for onward travel, and you'll have to indicate where you'll be staying on St Lucia, although this doesn't mean you can't move to different accommodation. For **enquiries**, call the St Lucia immigration department (see p.19) or St Lucian embassies or consulates in your own country.

St Lucian embassies and high commissions abroad

Canada 130 Albert Street, Suite 700, Ottawa, Ontario K1P 5G4, Canada ℡613/236 8952, ℻613/236 3042, ℯechcc@travel-net.com.

UK 1 Collingham Gardens, London SW5 0HW, ℡020/7370 7123, ℻020/7370 1905, ℯhcslu@btconnect.com.

US 3216 New Mexico Ave NW, Washington DC 20016 ℡202/364-6792, ℻202/364-6723, ℯeofsaintlu@aol.com.

There is no St Lucian diplomatic representation in Australia, New Zealand or Ireland.

For details of foreign embassies and consulates in St Lucia, see p.218.

Information, websites and maps

The St Lucia Tourist Board maintains several offices abroad, and it's worth contacting them to pick up general information and free maps before you leave. For the best on-island information, contact the main office of the **St Lucia Tourist Board** at the Sureline Building, just after the roundabout on your way north from Castries (PO Box 221, Castries, St Lucia, WI ⓣ 452-4094 or 452-5968, ⓕ 453-1121, ⓦ www.stlucia.org). There are also tourist board kiosks at George F.L. Charles Airport, the La Place Carenage and Pointe Seraphine shopping complexes in Castries (see p.58, p.65 and p.66), at Hewanorra airport (see p.115) in Vieux Fort, and at the waterfront in Soufrière (see p.105).

Other useful sources of up-to-date local information are the free, visitor-oriented publications available from the tourist board and from hotels across the island. *Tropical Traveller* is a monthly publication geared towards tourists, with lots of articles and suggestions for things to do as well as restaurant and nightclub listings, while the glossy magazine *Visions*, published by the St Lucia Hotel and Tourism Association, offers more of the same with the addition of hotel listings. It's also worth browsing the **internet** for island information, and we've recommended some of the most useful sites below.

Though tourist offices (and even car rental companies) will provide adequate **maps** of St Lucia, you may get a more useful and detailed map from suppliers at home. The best available is the 1:50,000 Ordnance Survey tourist map, available from bookshops or map specialists. In the UK, try Stanfords, 12–14 Long Acre, London, WC2E 9LP (for mail order call ☏020/7836 1321 or see ⓦwww.stanfords.co.uk), and in the US, try Rand McNally (for mail order or your nearest outlet call ☏1-800/275-7263 or log on to ⓦwww.randmcnally.com).

St Lucian Tourist offices abroad

Canada 8 King St East, Suite 700, Toronto, Ontario M5C 1B5 ☏416/362-4242 or 1–800-869-0377, ⓕ362-7832, ⓔSLTBcanada@aol.com.

UK 421a Finchley Rd, London NW3 6HJ, ☏020 7431 3675, ⓕ020 7431 7920.

US 800 2nd Ave, 9th Floor, New York, NY 10017 ☏1-800/456-3984 or 212/867-2950, ⓕ212/867-2795, ⓔStluciatourism@aol.com.

Websites

Ethnologue: St Lucia
ⓦwww.ethnologue.com/show_language.asp?code=DOM. Discussion of St Lucian Creole, its origins and its relation to other Caribbean French-based Patois languages.

Government of St Lucia
ⓦwww.stlucia.gov.lc. All the statistics you'd ever want to know, plus government news.

St Lucia Hotel and Tourism Association
ⓦwww.stluciatravel.com.lc. The official site of the SLHTA, including a long list of hotels and restaurants, duty-free shops and activities, as well as current weather reports.

St Lucia Jazz Festival
ⓦwww.stluciajazz.org. Listings of yearly line-ups with

artist biographies, news, current schedules and information on hotels and travel.

St Lucia One Stop

ⓦ www.sluonestop.com. Lively site with a chat room, searchable St Lucia phone directory and links to local newspapers.

St Lucia Tourist Board

ⓦ www.stlucia.org. The best general site, with history and travel facts as well as information on activities, hotels, restaurants, tourist office contacts on the island and overseas, and tips for those planning a St Lucian wedding.

Health and insurance

Visitors to St Lucia are unlikely to suffer any real health problems. Tap water is usually safe to drink, except in the immediate aftermath of hurricanes and heavy rains, when the potable water supply can be contaminated. In any case, inexpensive bottled water is available in supermarkets and shops. Under no circumstances should you drink river water – it might be okay, but assume that it's not. Bilharzia, a blood fluke that can cause serious liver, spleen and artery damage, has been found in rivers and streams on the island.

Your main health risk is probably the **tropical sun**, which is extremely strong, even on cloudy days. A wide-brimmed hat and strong sunscreen will help protect you, and if you are light-skinned and plan on snorkelling for any length of time, wearing a good-quality T-shirt (UV rays can penetrate thin clothing) will guard against overexposing your back. To avoid dehydration and sunstroke, you should aim to drink at least four litres of water per day, and keep covered up with light cotton clothing while out hiking or exploring, especially between 11am and 3pm, when the sun is at its strongest.

Dengue fever has recently made its way to St Lucia, where it is carried by the *Aedes aegypti* mosquito, which breeds in containers containing still water – coconut shells, old tires, drums, flower vases, etc. The Dengue fever virus is injected into humans by the bite of an infected mosquito. The disease can be extremely debilitating, but is easily treat-able. If you experience fever, intense headache, eye pain and joint and muscle pain, consult a medical professional. For more information, contact the St Lucian Ministry of Health on ☏758/451-9892.

The only other risk that travellers are likely to encounter are the poisonous **manchineel trees** with their shiny, green leaves, widespread along St Lucian shorelines. These should be treated with extreme caution as both the fruit, resembling a small, yellow apple, and the milky sap are toxic. Avoid touching any part of the tree or even taking cover under its boughs during a rain shower – the runoff can cause burns. Most hotels have labelled manchineels on their grounds.

AIDS is prevalent in St Lucia, making it extremely foolish to engage in unsafe sex. However, despite health education programmes, taboos still exist regarding condom use and other safe-sex practices. You can buy condoms on the island, but as they may have been sitting on shelves for a while, it's advisable to bring your own.

If you are unfortunate enough to need **medical help** in St Lucia, there are hospitals and health clinics throughout the island, but they are likely to be crowded and the facilities limited. Most large hotels can also recommend a doctor.

Details of hospitals, medical centres and pharmacies in St Lucia are given on p.219.

INSURANCE

It's a good idea to take out **travel insurance** before you leave for St Lucia, preferably a policy that covers medical treatment (including evacuation), theft and loss of baggage. Most travel agents and tour operators will offer you insurance when you book your flight or holiday, but it pays to shop around and check what coverage you may already have from your own health insurance. Home insurance policies may cover theft or loss whilst overseas, and private medical insurance may also be valid abroad; if this applies, make sure that you know how to make a claim. If you plan to indulge in **watersports** such as scuba diving, you'll often pay a higher premium, and it might be more difficult to find an appropriate policy. Also, bear in mind that some insurance companies will not cover **travellers over 65**, and those that do are likely to charge hefty premiums.

Note that in the event of a medical emergency you'll need a police report to make an insurance claim. Also, you will have to pay for any small medical bills and be re-imbursed at home, so be sure to keep receipts.

HEALTH AND INSURANC

25

ROUGH GUIDES TRAVEL INSURANCE

Rough Guides offers its own travel insurance, customized for our readers by a leading UK broker and backed by a Lloyd's underwriter. It's available for anyone, of any nationality and any age, travelling anywhere in the world.

There are two main Rough Guide insurance plans: Essential, for basic, no-frills cover; and Premier – with more generous and extensive benefits. Alternatively, you can take out annual multi-trip insurance, which covers you for any number of trips throughout the year (with a maximum of 60 days for any one trip). Unlike many policies, the Rough Guides schemes are calculated by the day, so if you're travelling for 27 days rather than a month, that's all you pay for. If you intend to be away for the whole year, the Adventurer policy will cover you for 365 days. Each plan can be supplemented with a "Hazardous Activities Premium" if you plan to indulge in sports considered dangerous, such as skiing, scuba-diving or trekking.

For a policy quote, call the Rough Guide Insurance Line on UK freefone ☎0800/015 0906, US toll-free ☎1-866/220 5588, or, if you're calling from elsewhere ☎+44 1243/621 046. Alternatively, get an online quote or buy online at ⓦwww.roughguidesinsurance.com.

Getting around

How easy you'll find it to get around St Lucia depends very much on where you want to go. While the more populated parts of the island – the west coast, for example – are well connected by buses, the northwest coast around Pointe du Cap and the east coast north of Dennery, where roads are poor, are only accessible to those with their own transport.

If you're laid-back enough to cope with waiting time and frequent stops along the route, travelling by bus is probably the most convenient and economical way to get around, with fares averaging out at EC$9 or less. An alternative is to rent taxis, though fares can soon add up.

The ideal way to traverse the island is, of course, to rent a **car**. As well as giving you complete independence, it's ultimately less expensive than taxi travel if you intend to do much exploring. If a car is beyond your budget, though, and you have the nerve, renting a **motorbike** is worth considering, though this isn't exactly the safest way to get around. To drive a car or ride a motorbike on the island, visitors must purchase a temporary St Lucian **licence**. Valid for three months, these cost EC$54 (US$21) and are issued by rental companies, the immigration departments at the airports and any island police department on production of a valid licence (or an international permit) from your own country of origin. Remember that in St Lucia, you drive on the **left side** of the road.

In and around Castries, Soufrière and Marigot Bay, you can also take advantage of the convenient and fun **water taxi** system, mostly used by tourists and especially handy for getting to nearby beaches.

In addition to the organized sporting activities listed elsewhere in this guide (see Chapter 10), several companies offer unique **tours** of the island, which may be worth considering if time is short.

BUSES

Identifiable by an "H" on the licence plate, St Lucia's **buses** are small vans whose customized windscreens are emblazoned with colourful names such as "Tempt Me" or "Redemption". Though all of the island's buses are privately owned, **fares** are set by the government and are inexpensive: you'll pay no more than EC$10 to travel between any two points on the island. Castries to the north costs around EC$2.50, Castries to Vieux Fort is EC$8.50. Schedules are less predictable, though, with most drivers waiting until the bus is full before setting off; as a general rule, services between major towns run every thirty to sixty minutes from about 6am until 10pm on weekdays, with an extended timetable on Fridays for the Gros Islet jump-up and a reduced timetable on Saturdays; practically no buses run on Sundays. Small cement pavilions serve as **bus stops**, but if you flag a bus down anywhere along a route, it will probably stop if it isn't jammed full.

In **Castries**, all the main bus stops are located in the downtown area. Services **north** to Gros Islet and Cap Estate (route 1A) leave from the Anglican School on Darling Road. For Vieux Fort and the **south** via the east

SAMPLE BUS FARES

Soufrière to: Vieux Fort EC$7.50
Soufrière to: Castries along the west coast road EC$8.50
Vieux Fort to: Castries EC$8.50

Buses also make runs along the west coast from Marigot, Anse la Raye and Canaries to Castries, and you'll pay less than EC$7 to get to the capital.

coast (route 2H), head to the stop at the junction of Jean-Baptiste Street and Darling Road, while **Soufrière** buses (route 3D) leave from Carl's Crescent. Anse la Raye and **Marigot** buses (route 3C) depart from Victoria Street between Chaussee Road and Chisel Street, for **Morne Fortune** (route 5F) from St Louis Street between Coral and Peynier Streets and for **Dennery**, **Praslin** and **Mon Repos** (route 2D) from the Micoud Street junction.

In **Vieux Fort**, buses to Castries (route 4B) leave from New Dock Road on the south side of the airport, while the stand for west coast buses to Soufrière (route 4A) is also south of the airport at Clarke Street, next to a traffic light and a Shell service station.

TAXIS

Taxis – identifiable by their red licence plates with the letters "TX" – are usually mini vans seating 6-8 people and are in plentiful supply. You'll see them cruising for fares on the streets of the main towns, and at obvious locations such as airports and tourist spots like Pigeon Island and Reduit Beach. Though all taxis are unmetered, **fares** are expensive and set by the government, and drivers are required to carry a rate sheet in their car. While most drivers stick to the already overblown set rates, it's always best to confirm

SAMPLE TAXI FARES

George F.L. Charles Airport to: downtown Castries EC$15, Rodney Bay EC$35, Cap Estate EC$50, Vieux Fort EC$140.
Downtown Castries to: Soufrière EC$160, Anse la Raye EC$65.
Hewanorra International Airport to: Soufrière EC$150, downtown Castries EC$140, Gros Islet EC$180.

the fare before getting in. Taxis also offer **guided tours** for around US$20 per hour (for as many as four people), or US$140 for a full day, but unlike standard fares, this rate is often negotiable.

CAR RENTAL

Car rental **rates** start at US$45 per day for a compact, manual-shift vehicle without air conditioning, and go as high as US$90 for a luxury model. Jeeps and other 4WD vehicles, which you'll need to explore some parts of the island, range from US$65 to US$100. You'll generally pay less during low season, or if you rent for three or more days. While mileage is unlimited, rates don't include **petrol**, which at time of writing cost around EC$8 per imperial gallon. Note that you need to be **aged 21** or over to rent a car, and some companies require a minimum age of 25.

Before you get into the rental vehicle, go over it with the attendant to ensure that the spare tyre is in good shape and there is a jack. Note that collision and liability **insurance** will cost as much as US$15 per day; however, certain credit cards allow you to waive the on-site insurance and remain covered as long as you pay for the rental using the card. Call your credit card company to enquire.

DRIVING IN ST LUCIA

As less than half of St Lucia's 800km of paved roads are on flat land, driving can be a challenge. The **west coast road** from Cap Estate in the north to Vieux Fort in the south has been vastly improved in recent years, but is full of twists and turns, steep hills and, during the rainy season, possible mudslides. Connecting Castries to Vieux Fort via Dennery, the **central and east coast highway** is in excellent shape and the quickest way to get from the south to the north of the island. In the **north**, the roads that link the east and west coasts are horrifically potholed at times, and often impassable without a 4WD vehicle. The same goes for roads in the **south** that head up into the central rainforests, which deteriorate the further you head into the interior. Driving in the **towns** is also challenging; all have a surfeit of one-way roads that are clogged with vehicles parked on both sides, and traffic jams are always imminent.

Signage is sporadic at best. Major turnoffs are usually marked, but some signs have faded. Many roads don't have names at all but are known as the "road to Cas-en-Bas" and so on, but you should be able to find your way if armed with a good road map (see p.22).

Car rental companies

Avis Castries ⓣ 452-4554, Hewanorra airport ⓣ 454-6325, George F.L. Charles Airport ⓣ 452-2046; ⓦ www.avis.com.

Budget/Sunset Motors Castries ⓣ 452-0233, Hewanorra airport ⓣ 454-5311; ⓦ www.budgetslucia.com.

Cool Breeze Soufrière ⓣ 459-7729 and four other airport locations; ⓦ coolbreeze carrental.com/stlucia/.

Courtesy Gros Islet ⓣ 452-8140; ⓦ www.stluciatravel.com.lc/courtesyrentals.htm.

Guy's Gablewoods Mall ⓣ 451-7147, ⓔ guysltd@hotmail.com.

Hertz Hewanorra airport ⓣ 454-9636, George F.L. Charles Airport ⓣ 451-7351; ⓦ www.stluciatravel.com.lc/hertz.htm.

Vacation & Corporate Car Rentals Castries ⓣ 452 9404, ⓕ 450 2272; ⓔ vcrental @hotmail.com.

MOTORBIKE RENTAL

Though it is possible to get around St Lucia on a **motorbike**, it's obviously less safe than a car, and you'll have to watch out for hazards that you might not encounter at home, such as torrential tropical rain, large potholes and lazy animals sunbathing in the middle of the roads. You won't have space for much luggage, and wearing a heavy helmet in the heat can be uncomfortable – St Lucian riders rarely use them. Having said that, motorcycles and scooters are certainly less expensive than cars, starting at US$30 per day for bikes in the 250–550cc range – you'll also have to obtain the three-month temporary driver's licence required by all foreigners renting vehicles on the island (see p.27). Wayne's Motorcycle Centre, just north of Castries (ⓣ 452-2059), is the island's only motorbike **rental outlet**.

WATER TAXIS

Generally small wooden boats that carry no more than four passengers, many of St Lucia's **water taxis** (ⓣ 454-5420) are in fact fishing boats moonlighting for extra cash. In the **Soufrière** area, where a water taxi association acts as a dispatcher (see p.104), boats carry passengers from the town's waterfront to many of the beaches in the area for about EC$25 one way – a quick and fun way to travel. Also on offer are forty-minute sightseeing trips to Castries (US$350 round-trip for four); a regular one-way trip to Castries for a minimum of four people costs US$90-100 for four. In

Castries harbour, water taxis ferry passengers (mainly from the cruise ships) between the Pointe Seraphine shopping complex and the downtown docks.

TOURS

Several local companies offer conventional **guided tours** of St Lucia's east coast and central mountains, aboard big, brightly painted and quite obviously tourist-filled 4WD trucks. Most are all-day, all-inclusive expeditions averaging at a hefty US$80-90 per person, with stops at waterfalls, high-mountain viewing areas and beaches; some involve rainforest hikes of up to three hours. Lunch, refreshments and admission to selected sites are part of the deal, and you are picked up at your hotel. You won't be part of an intimate group, however – some companies set out with as many as forty people. For more information, contact Jungle Tours in Castries (☎ 450-0434, ℱ 450-9154, ⓦ www.jungletoursstlucia.com) or Sunlink Jeep Safaris in Rodney Bay (☎ 452-8232, ⓦ www.sunlinktours.com).

A more adventurous option is the inland and coastal **guided walks** offered by the St Lucia National Trust (☎ 452-5005, ⓦ www.slunatrust.org) and the Forest and Lands Department (☎ 450-2231 or 450-2375, ⓦ www.slumaffe.org). The Trust offer walking tours of the Fregate and Maria Islands nature reserves, the arid Pointe Hardy area (see p.95) and the Morne Fortune historic sites (see p.75) for between EC$48 and EC$90 per person, excluding bus travel (up to EC$25). Be warned, however, that these walks are not always available, so call ahead.

Hiking routes in the interior are covered in Chapter 6.

The Forest and Lands Department concentrate on the hiking trails within the interior **forest reserves**, and hiring one of their guides is mandatory if you want to enter certain protected parts of the central rainforest. Popular treks include the Edmund Forest (see p.144) cross-island hike, and the Barre de L'Isle or Des Cartier rainforest trails (see p.143 and p.147). You pay a flat EC$25 per person for entry to each trail and for the services of a guide, but again, the Forestry Department isn't a professional tour company: ranger stations at the start of trails are not consistently staffed, so it's not always easy to find a forestry guide on site.

Lastly, breathtaking but exorbitantly priced **aerial tours** of the island are offered by St Lucia Helicopters (⊤ 453-6950, ⓕ 452-1553) from their base at Pointe Seraphine in Castries. The ten-minute northern excursion passes over the west coast and Pigeon Island, as well as the north Atlantic shore, and costs around US$45 per person. A twenty-minute southern tour over Soufrière and the central mountains is around US$85, and a thirty-minute jaunt around the entire island runs at about US$120 per person.

Costs, money and banks

Like most of the Caribbean, St Lucia isn't an inexpensive place to visit. In restaurants and supermarkets, costs are similar to those in the US or Europe and the cheapest eating options are usually the local fish and vegetable markets or roadside stands set up in just about every town and village.

When it comes to **budgeting**, accommodation is likely to be your major expense, with the most expensive time during the busy mid-December to mid-April high season. For the large upscale properties, expect to pay at least US$250 per night in the high season, and US$120 for smaller hotels. Throw in a rental car for US$50 per day, and you're talking serious money. However, if you stay in guesthouses (US$10–25 per night), limit yourself to travelling by bus and eat at smaller local restaurants, you can happily get by on US$30 per day.

CURRENCY AND EXCHANGE RATES

St Lucia's official currency is the **Eastern Caribbean dollar** (EC$), which is also legal tender in Anguilla, Antigua and Barbuda, Dominica, Grenada, Montserrat, St Kitts and Nevis and St Vincent and the Grenadines. Bills come in denominations of EC$100, EC$50, EC$20, EC$10 and EC$5, and there are 50, 25, 10, 5 and 1 cent coins as well as an EC$1 coin. The EC dollar trades against the US dollar at an official rate of EC$2.68 to US$1 for travellers' cheque exchanges, slightly less for cash conversions. This rate has remained stable for years, and only ever varies by a few cents.

In the case of hotels, car rental, restaurants and practically everything related to tourism, most **prices** in St Lucia are quoted in both EC and US dollars, and occasionally only in the latter. In effect, the **US dollar** serves as the island's unofficial currency, and you can use US bills freely in virtually any transaction, though your change will always be in EC currency. Note that ATM machines only dispense EC dollars.

In this guide, we have endeavoured to quote prices in EC dollars or US dollars as appropriate (for example, EC$ for bus fares and US$ for airfares). However, be aware that on the street, the most common exchange rate is EC$2.50 to US$1, which goes in the vendor's favour – a taxi fare of EC$25 is equal to US$10, not the US$9.30 you'd calculate using the official exchange rate.

CREDIT CARDS AND TRAVELLERS' CHEQUES

Major **credit cards** such as Visa, American Express and MasterCard, are widely accepted for payment (the Discover Card is less recognized), and you can also use them to obtain **cash advances** in banks. The island's Royal Bank of Canada **ATMs** accept Cirrus and Plus cards, as well as Visa and MasterCard. Machines are located on William Peter Boulevard in Castries, at the Rodney Bay Marina, and on New Dock Road in Vieux Fort. The Caribbean Banking

Corporation ATMs at Micoud Street in downtown Castries and Gablewoods Mall, north of town, take the same cards.

US dollar **travellers' cheques** are accepted by many businesses, but it's wise to always carry some cash with you, as taxi drivers, market stalls and many smaller restaurants or guesthouses won't accept credit cards or travellers' cheques.

BANKS AND EXCHANGE

Banks are found in all major towns on the island, with the majority located in Castries. **Opening hours** are Monday to Thursday from 8am to 3pm, and Friday from 8am to 5pm. The National Commercial Bank exchange bureau at Hewanorra airport in Vieux Fort is open later than most, and has weekend hours (Mon–Tues 12.30–9pm, Wed 4.30–9pm, Thurs 2–9pm, Fri 12.30–9pm, Sat 2.30–9pm & Sun 1–9pm), and the Royal Bank of Canada branch at the Rodney Bay Marina is open from 8am to noon each Saturday. Banks always offer the most favourable **exchange rate** – while hotels are more convenient, you'll usually get slightly less for your money.

For details of bank branches in St Lucia, see p.217.

TAXES AND TIPPING

Hotels in St Lucia will almost always add two extra charges to their bills that may not be included in quoted room rates: a ten percent **service charge** and an eight percent government **accommodation tax**. These can bring your bill up an alarming eighteen percent – a hefty addition for a week's stay even at a medium-priced hotel – so it's well worth checking whether taxes are included in the price before you book.

Remember that you must pay a EC$54 (US$22) departure tax when leaving St Lucia by air, and an EC$20 tax if you depart by ferry.

Restaurants often add a ten percent **service charge** onto the bill as well. In theory, this is designed to be a tip for waiting staff, but in many cases it never reaches their pockets. To compensate, you could leave an extra five percent at a restaurant. Similarly, if you want to be sure your chambermaid gets a tip, leave an extra couple of dollars for each night you've stayed. Cab drivers should be paid ten percent; porters EC$0.50 a bag.

Communications

All major towns and villages have a post office; the major ones in Anse La Raye, Castries, Dennery, Gros Islet, Micoud, Soufrière and Vieux Fort are open Monday to Friday between 8.15am and 4.30pm, while the smaller offices only open between 1pm and 5pm. The General Post Office on Bridge Street in Castries (☎452-

5157) is the island's largest and has a philatelic bureau. Sending postcards and packages to the US, Canada or Europe costs less than EC$1, but as they can take up to two weeks to reach their destination, you might want to send urgent items home via the courier services that have offices in Castries: FedEx are on Derek Walcott Square (☏452-1320), DHL are on Manoel Street (☏453-1538), and UPS on Bridge Street (☏452-7211). Costs vary according to destination and weight, but you can be assured it will be at least ten times the postal rate.

When addressing a letter to St Lucia, include
"West Indies" after the name and address.

St Lucia's **phone system** is reliable. Public phone booths are located all around the island and take either **coins** (EC$1 or EC$0.25) or the **phone cards** available from Cable & Wireless offices (see below), post offices, pharmacies, souvenir stores and convenience shops. Phone cards come in denominations of EC$40, EC$20 and EC$10. **Local calls** cost EC$0.25 for two minutes, double that for long-distance.

To call St Lucia from overseas, use your country's
international access code (001 in UK, Ireland and NZ, 1
in the US and Canada, 00111 from Australia), followed
by area code 758 and the seven-digit number.

You can send faxes and telegrams and make phone calls – at substantially cheaper rates than those offered by hotels – from the Cable & Wireless offices in Castries, Gablewoods Mall and Vieux Fort (all Mon–Fri 8am–6.30pm, Sat 8am–12.30pm). **Internet** access is currently limited to these Cable & Wireless offices, where it costs a reasonable

COMMUNICATIONS

EC\$5 for thirty minutes, and most of the bigger hotels, many of which allow access to guests only, and charge extortionate prices for the privilege.

The media

St Lucia's newspapers provide the lowdown on local news as well as up-to-date entertainment information. The island's main titles are the *Star* (Ⓦwww.stluciastar.com), the *Voice* and the *St Lucia Mirror*, all tabloid size. The *Voice* was established in 1885, making it one of the oldest newspapers in the region. The three carry much of the same information, mainly focusing on the local political scene, along with some international news and a big sports section. The entertainment section of the *Voice* is good for local events, while the *Star* tends to be the more complete all-around hard news organ. There's also a regional weekend newspaper, *One Caribbean* (Ⓦwww .onecaribbean.com), serving Grenada, Dominica, St Lucia, and St Vincent. The *Crusader* is a free paper with some news and local events, available at bookstores, grocery stores and shops.

You can hear local news and current events listings on St Lucia's several AM and FM **radio** stations, among them Gem Radio (94.5 FM), Radio Caribbean (101.1 FM), Radio St Lucia (97.7 FM, 660 AM), and Radio100 Helen (100.1 FM). Of the lot, Radio St Lucia carries more news and talk, while Gem and Radio100 Helen provide a mix of international and local music.

Mid-range and upscale hotels generally have access to satellite-fed international cable **television** stations, including HBO and some British and French channels. On channels four and five, the local stations **HTS** (Helen Television System, ⓦwww.htsstluica.com) and **DTS** offer news and sports broadcasts, local talk shows and some original programmes.

Safety, harassment and drugs

Generally, St Lucia is a safe place for visitors. The usual precautions for avoiding theft are in order, but the worst that most visitors are likely to encounter is some harassment, though even this is usually confined to areas where tourists congregate in numbers, such as the entrance to Pigeon Island, Soufrière waterfront and Reduit Beach. For women travelling alone, however, harassment can be more of an issue.

PERSONAL SAFETY

Petty **theft** is on the increase and occasional robberies are reported, so it's wise to employ the common sense practices you follow at home. Don't leave your belongings unattended on the beach – ask someone to watch them while you take a dip; avoid public beaches late at night (the moon might be out, and so might a few thugs); carry your wallet or purse in a pouch or front pocket rather than an open bag; and avoid pulling out large wads of cash when shopping in the street or market. If you've got a rental car, never leave valuables in plain view, and always lock the doors when you leave it. Lastly, it's sensible to check for "H" plates on all vehicles declaring themselves taxis.

If you are unlucky enough to have something stolen or an offence is committed against you, you should contact the local police immediately, and if you want to make an insurance claim, you'll need to get a police report. Local officers are usually friendly and happy to help, though things may take a little longer than you're used to.

Details of embassies and consulates in St Lucia are listed on p.218.

Usually amounting to a few assertive vendors trying to make some money, **harassment** is a subjective problem. In St Lucia, it's not nearly as bad as in other Caribbean destinations, and is unlikely to ruin your trip or inhibit your interaction with St Lucians. However, as a tourist, you will inevitably be approached by people selling carvings, aloe sunburn treatments, T-shirts or hair-braiding services, particularly in heavily visited parts of the island such as Reduit Beach, Castries Central Market, Soufrière waterfront and the streets of Gros Islet during the Friday night street party. A firm but respectful "no, thank you" usually works, much like it should.

Police stations in St Lucia

Castries ☎ 452-2372
Choiseul ☎ 459-3233
Dennery ☎ 453-4277
Gros Islet & Rodney Bay
☎ 452-8155

Soufrière ☎ 459-7333
Vieux Fort ☎ 454-6333

Emergency numbers

Police ☎ 999
Fire and ambulance ☎ 911
Victoria Hospital, Castries
☎ 452-2421

SAFETY, HARASSMENT AND DRUGS

DRUGS

Though **drugs** are available, they are of course **illegal** in St Lucia, where the vigorous anti-drugs stance includes occasional sweeps of areas where such substances are known to be handled, such as the Gros Islet street party. **Crack cocaine** and **marijuana** are the most common narcotics, and increased use by island youths has led to police consternation and crackdowns; officers often work undercover. Always bear in mind that St Lucia is a small island. If you buy drugs, only you and the dealer – and about thirty other people – will know instantly, and one of them may owe a favour to the local authorities. As a rule, visitors should be extra wary of drug use in St Lucia; prosecutions of foreigners are not unknown, and you do not want to spend time in a St Lucian lock-up.

WOMEN TRAVELLERS

By and large, **women** travelling to St Lucia alone stand the chance of incurring some harassment or, at the very least, lively interest in their solo status. In the beaches and resort areas, you'll find that some men will circle about like airplanes waiting for permission to land. Most of the time, this is irritating rather than threatening, but there's always a small chance that a situation could turn nasty.

To minimize potential problems, it's important not to cast aside your common sense just because you feel like you're in paradise. Don't contemplate going to the Gros Islet street party on your own, don't sunbathe alone on secluded beaches, head off into the rainforest with a stranger or traipse off to the market in a bikini, and always trust your instincts. Regardless of the cultural backgrounds involved, flirtations are easily assessed; if you think a man is interested, he probably is. Bear in mind that women who've visited

St Lucia before you have set the precedent, and some were actively seeking sexual encounters. If you're not interested, be very clear about it – a firm "no" works most of the time. It's also a good idea to develop a sense of humour concerning the whole business of come-ons; most of it probably has more to do with your perceived economic status than your film-star looks. If you do feel a situation taking a turn for the worse, make a fuss and noise (much like St Lucian women do), and immediately head for a crowd.

Shopping

St Lucia is not brimming with opportunities for shopping, although those seeking duty-free items, crafts and art will find plenty to feed their appetites. Most shops open on weekdays between 8.30am and 12.30pm, and from 1.30 to 4.30pm, and on Saturdays from 8.30am to 12.30pm. Shops at Gablewoods Mall, just north of Castries, stay open until 8pm on weekdays and Saturdays, 1pm on Sundays; Pointe Seraphine duty-free shops stay open until 2pm on Saturday. Very few stores keep Sunday hours, though you may find some open if there's a cruise ship moored at Port Castries.

Gablewoods Mall is a good all-round place for some shopping, with some thirty shops ranging from chemists to supermarkets to craft shops, as well as bank branches, a post office and several restaurants.

DUTY-FREE SHOPPING

As the island's cruise ship destination, Castries is your best bet for **duty-free** shopping. The **Pointe Seraphine** complex (see p.66) on the north side of the harbour has 25 outlets that stock jewellery, watches, crystal, perfumes, sunglasses, clothing, cigars and electronics as well as stores selling touristy items and souvenirs such as coconut carvings, T-shirts and beach wear. Across the harbour from Pointe Seraphine and reachable via a shuttle ferry, the **La Place Carenage** duty-free centre at the North Wharf on Jeremie Street is a smaller branch of Pointe Seraphine.

Although the term "duty-free" implies that the vendor has not paid import duty on its goods and is therefore in a position to pass on its savings to the consumer, this isn't always the case, and you may not always be making a saving. To ensure you get a good deal, it's best to have an idea of what potential purchases would cost at home, and compare prices. Also, don't forget that duty-free items are subject to customs allowances in your own country.

CRAFTS AND SOUVENIRS

Crafts are on sale throughout the island, and browsing around the markets and shops is half the fun of a craft-buying excursion. A wide range of inexpensive carvings, paintings, T-shirts and the like are sold at **Castries'** Central Market and the Vendor's Arcade, downtown on Jeremie and

Peynier streets respectively. Prices are good and craft items range from occasionally tacky carvings or straw baskets to intricate wood sculptures. In **Soufrière**, stop at the Crafts Centre at the north end of the waterfront walkway for an inexpensive and varied selection of souvenirs; also in the southwest, the Choiseul Arts and Craft Centre (℡459-3226) is the island's premier local outlet. Their pottery, mats, carvings, wicker baskets and traditional wood furniture are high quality and reasonably priced. Bright island-style **clothing**, wraps and beach wear are the hallmarks of Bagshaw Studios (℡452-6039) out on the La Toc Road south of Castries and with branches at Pointe Seraphine, Hewanorra and Castries Northern waterfront, and of Caribelle Batik (℡452-3785) in Morne Fortune – there's also a branch at Gablewoods Mall and one at Rodney Bay (℡452-8728).

ART

St Lucia's **art galleries** include Eudovic Art Studio on Morne Fortune (℡452-2747; see p.76), where you can buy original sculptures and watch artisans at work; Artsibit on Brazil Street in Castries (℡452-7865), which displays works by local artists; and the gallery owned by renowned local artist Llewellyn Xavier, St Lucia Fine Art, at Pointe Seraphine (℡459 0891), which has a large collection of his oils on canvas and prints.

MARKETS AND SUPERMARKETS

Shopping for fresh fruits, vegetables and fish at **local markets** such as the main Central Market in Castries, and the dozens of smaller markets around the island, is the best way to save money and have fun doing it. **Bargaining** is not a blood sport in St Lucia, but you can banter nicely about prices with the vendor, and will often get a better deal; bear in mind, though, that a "heap" of mangoes, for instance, meaning about eight fruits, is EC$1, hardly a price worth sweating over. Shopping at **supermarkets** is another way to save on eating costs, and those listed below have good selections of fresh fruits and vegetables, bakery items, meats and deli fare.

For more on St Lucian food, see p.176.

Supermarkets

Julian's Supermarket
Gablewoods Mall, Sunny
Acres (Mon–Thurs 8am–8pm,
Fri & Sat 8am–9pm,
Sun 9am–1pm) and
Gablewoods Mall South,
Vieux Fort. Mon–Thurs
8am–8pm, Fri & Sat
8am–9pm, Sun 8am–1pm.

Glace Supermarket Marisule,
Castries (Mon–Sat 8am–8pm,
Sun 8am–noon).

JQ Supermarket Bridge St,
Castries (Mon–Wed
8am–6pm, Thurs 8am–7pm,
Fri 8am–8pm, Sat 8am–4pm)
and Rodney Bay Mall.
Mon–Thurs 8am–10pm, Fri &
Sat 8am–12am, Sun
8am–4pm.

Festivals and public holidays

Of St Lucia's roster of festivals and public holidays, the main events are the St Lucia Jazz Festival, an international-class event held at various venues islandwide in May, and the July Carnival, a joyful mishmash of street parades, costume competitions and monumental parties. Unless otherwise indicated, more information and specific

PUBLIC HOLIDAYS

January 1 New Year's Day
February 22 Independence Day
March/April Good Friday & Easter Monday
May 1 Labour Day
Seventh Monday after Easter Whit Monday

First Monday in August Emancipation Day
October 25 Thanksgiving Day
November 1 All Saints' Day
November 2 All Souls' Day
December 13 National Day
December 25 Christmas Day
December 26 Boxing Day

dates for all events listed in this section can be obtained from the St Lucia tourist board offices on the island and worldwide; the tourist board website, ⓦ www.stlucia.org, is also a good source of information on new events.

Visitors should note that on public holidays (see below) most government offices, tourist information kiosks and shops are closed, while the majority of tourist attractions remain open.

ANNUAL EVENTS

February

Independence Day on February 22 commemorates the original 1979 ceremony, with political speeches and parades.

April

Earth Day celebrations, sponsored by the National Trust (ⓣ 452-5005, ⓦ www.slunatrust .org), take place on April 22. A predawn climb to Pigeon Island to watch buglers from the police band regale the rising sun is just part of the fun.

May

The Festival of Comedy (ⓣ 452-5005, ⓦ www.slunatrust .org) is the St Lucia National Trust's annual fundraiser and comprises two nights of local comedy acts and theatre at the Cultural Centre in Castries and Pigeon Island usually in early May. Tourists are welcome, though some plays might be in difficult-to-understand Patois.

The four-day St Lucia International Jazz Festival (ⓦ www.stluciajazz.org) swings into action in early or mid-may at the Cultural Centre on the outskirts of Castries, at Pigeon Island and at various spots around the country, including some smaller, more intimate venues in the south (see p.198).

June

Walk for the Environment takes place on World Environment Day (June 5) and is sponsored by the National Trust (see opposite).

The **Feast of St Peter** (also called the Fishermen's Feast Day) takes place on June 29, and involves religious services and the blessing of fishing boats. It is particularly well attended in Dennery, a mainstay of the industry.

July

Steeped in St Lucia's strong French and Roman Catholic traditions, one of the most popular annual festivities is **Carnival** (see p.199), comprising costumed street parades, calypso music and general partying in the Castries area during the first half of July.

August

Christianity has brought saint's day celebrations to St Lucia, such as La Rose on August 30, also called the **Feast of Rose De Lima**. Micoud is a well-known hot-spot for the festivities, but island-wide activities include religious services, flower shows, costume parades, balls, feasts and performances of traditional song and dance.

October

Held in late October, **Jounen Kweyol Entenasyonnal** (International Creole Day) sees Creole-language islands celebrating their language and culture through music, storytelling and dance. In St Lucia, most events take place in Castries. October is also Creole Heritage Month.

La Marguerite (Feast of St Margaret Mary Alacoque) on October 17 honours the saint with religious services, sports activities and folk performances.

November

November 22, **St Cecilia's Day** is a celebration of the saint of musicians, also known as the Feast of Musicians and feted with performances of traditional folk music alongside more modern jazz and calypso.

December

National Day on December 13 is also the **Feast of St Lucy**, marked by island-wide cultural festivals and sports activities such as boat races and football games. St Lucia's Christmas festivities also commence on this day.

THE GUIDE

THE GUIDE

Castries
and around

Home to some sixty thousand people (more than a third of the island's population), St Lucia's capital of **CASTRIES**, on the northwest coast, is a metaphor for contemporary West Indian urban culture: at times busy and congested, at times sleepy and peaceful, the town feels stuck between a centuries-old West Indian lifestyle and a desperate push to modernize. The capital's appearance is thoroughly modern, with the areas around the waterfront and government complex in particular featuring gleaming structures of glass, concrete and steel. The classic West Indian look of brightly painted wood and intricate ginger-bread fretwork has largely been lost over the years due to several major **fires** destroying the original colonial buildings.

Despite its contemporary feel, Castries retains a certain unaffected charm, largely due to its setting – the town is wrapped around the deep harbour of **Port Castries** where each year hundreds of cruise ships dock to unload credit-card toting tourists for a day of duty-free shopping at the city's malls. Spreading back from the harbour, the compact

downtown area consists of a dozen or so blocks of busy streets, shops and bus stands, as well as a few interesting monuments and the bustling **Castries Central Market**, a rich mix of colour, aroma and noise. You'll only need a short time to see the capital, as it isn't particularly blessed with museums, historical sights or cultural venues; most visitors are here for business or shopping rather than sightseeing.

North of downtown and across the harbour, John Compton Highway, lined with government offices, leads toward **Vigie Peninsula**, a flat spit of partially reclaimed land which hosts the island's largest duty-free complex, **Pointe Seraphine**, as well as the small **George F.L. Charles Airport** and several hotels and waterfront restaurants.

With lovely beaches at **Choc Bay** further north, the forest-smothered **Morne Fortune** hills and lush banana fields in the south, the fascinating cultural coffer of the **Folk Research Centre** to the east and historic ruins like the well-preserved **La Toc Battery** just west, the area around Castries is well worth exploring. Even without a car, it's easy to get to all the sights thanks to the capital's good public transport links, and all of the sights and towns could be done as easy day trips. But as there are far more compelling accommodation options tucked into the hills surrounding the city, not to mention the occasional beach resort along the coast in either direction, you're probably much better off basing yourself outside rather than in the capital anyway.

The area covered in this chapter is shown in detail on maps 2 and 3, at the back of this book.

Some history

Though there are few physical traces, Castries is a veritable repository of St Lucia's **history**. In 1651, French settlers built a bastion on the peninsula now called Vigie, on the northern outskirts of the area that would become Castries. The settlement grew over the years, and by 1767 the population had shifted south to the banks of the river that flowed into the deep harbour known as Petit Cul de Sac by the French. The settlement was renamed in 1785 in honour of the Marquis de Castries, a minister of the French navy and one of the architects of French military efforts in the Caribbean.

The town has flourished as a **port** ever since, despite the successive fires and several disastrous hurricanes – not to mention the minor interruption of the French Revolution, which saw Republicans descend on the island to round up and execute selected members of the French nobility. Castries remained a busy port throughout nineteenth-century British rule, becoming an important **refuelling station** for coal-burning steamships on long ocean voyages, and a convenient stopover for massive cargo and military ships. The port expanded slowly, and new docks and piers were built throughout the twentieth century, some on reclaimed land. By the early twentieth century, Castries' population had burgeoned, and the streets were packed full of warehouses, homes and shacks – most made of wood and stacked alongside each other like matches in a box. As it turned out, the resemblance was more than physical. In May 1927, a large **fire** swept through the downtown area, destroying half the city, and in June 1948, another tremendous blaze levelled almost the entire town. Castries' recovery from these fires was swift, and today the city has settled into a comfortable existence as a mercantile port, tourist destination and seat of government.

Arrival, information and transport

St Lucia's small, regional **George F.L. Charles Airport** (℡452-1156) lies about a kilometre from downtown Castries on Vigie Peninsula, making the city a logical first stop if you arrive by **air** from another Caribbean island. There is a **tourist information** booth (open daily for all incoming flights; ℡452-2596) immediately outside the arrival doors, and a row of **car rental** kiosks (see p.30). Just outside the arrival area is a **taxi** stand (℡452-1599); the five-minute taxi ride to downtown costs EC$15.

While compact Castries is easy to navigate by **foot**, it is not an easy city to get around by **car** as the narrow streets can be congested, particularly on weekdays. However, **parking** is not a problem thanks to the new municipal multi-storey car park (EC$1.50/hr) opposite the Castries market, on the John Compton Highway as you come into town. Free parking is available at the car park outside the Marketing Board building behind the market on Jeremie Street and on the city outskirts (Pointe Seraphine is a good bet) – from here you can take a taxi or water taxi downtown (see opposite).

The capital is a public transport hub, with informal **bus** terminals scattered around town providing services to all areas of the island. There are several drop-off locations, including the Marketing Board, Jeremie Street, Darling Road, Peynier Street, Jean Baptiste Street, Micoud Street and Manoel Street. These are all downtown stops within walking distance of one other, close to all city transport.

For more on bus services from the capital, including details on how to get to the surrounding areas, see p.28.

If you're a passenger on a visiting **cruise** ship, you'll most likely disembark on the north side of Castries harbour, conveniently close to the Pointe Seraphine duty-free shopping complex (see p.66). At the back of the complex, a signposted jetty is the place to catch a **water taxi** for the five-minute ride to the North Wharf – also called Elizabeth II dock – in downtown Castries (US$1) from where it's a short walk southeast along Jeremie Street to buses, taxis and the rest of town. Boats cross the harbour every 30 to 45 minutes, more frequently when a cruise ship is docked.

Those arriving from Guadeloupe, Dominica or Martinique via the high-speed L'Express des Iles **ferry** (see p.18) disembark at the North Wharf.

INFORMATION

In addition to the tourist information booth at the airport (see opposite), the **St Lucia Tourist Board** has an administrative office on the second floor of the Sureline Building complex (⊤452-4094 or 452-5968, ⑤453-1121, ⑩www.stlucia.org) in Vide Bouteille, north of Castries on the road between the airport and Rodney Bay. However, visitors will find the **tourist information kiosk** downstairs at the Pointe Seraphine complex (Mon–Fri 8am–4.30pm; ⊤452-7577) much more useful and accessible as it remains open to accommodate cruise-ship visitors arriving outside regular opening hours. The kiosk stocks free maps, brochures and information about Castries and the rest of the island. There's also a kiosk near the La Place Carenage docks on Jeremie Street, opening mainly for cruise ship traffic.

Reviews of accommodation in and around Castries start on p.151; for eating and drinking listings, see p.175.

INFORMATION

Downtown Castries

A few notable monuments exist in the capital, which, along with the colourful market, can be seen in an afternoon. The focal point of downtown Castries, a fairly compact rectangle of streets, is **Derek Walcott Square**, which, with its fine architecture and central location, makes an ideal place to start any city tour. Lining the square to the south, **Brazil Street**'s handful of classic West Indian wooden buildings make an overly elegant backdrop to the constant stream of pedestrians and traffic, while to the east towers the **Cathedral of the Immaculate Conception**, the St Lucian showpiece of the Roman Catholic Church. To the north of the square, vendors at **Castries Central Market** hawk everything from coconuts to local crafts; there are some cheap, excellent food options here too, and the atmosphere is not to be missed.

DEREK WALCOTT SQUARE

Map 2, D6–E6.

Named after St Lucia's famous Nobel Prizewinning poet and playwright (see box on p.61), **Derek Walcott Square** is just southwest of Castries Central Market (see p.64). Though it's a peaceful spot today, the square has had a turbulent history. In the late eighteenth century following the French Revolution, it was known as the Place d'Armes, and a **guillotine** was set up here by Republicans anxious to do away with selected members of the nobility. It was then called Promenade Square, and later still Columbus Square (1892), before being given its present name in 1993. Bordered by bustling Brazil, Micoud, Bourbon and Laborie streets – the oldest and most attractive parts of the capital –

DEREK WALCOTT

Born on St Lucia in 1930, poet and playwright Derek Walcott was awarded the Nobel Prize for Literature in 1992. He remains one of the finest writers, Caribbean or otherwise, of recent times, a fervent proponent of the West Indian cultural and linguistic rhythms he employs and celebrates in his writing.

Educated at St Mary's College in Castries and at the University of the West Indies in Jamaica, his poetry was first published when he was just 18 and still a student. After moving to New York in the late 1950s, he attended acting school and, in 1959, established the Trinidad Theatre Workshop in Port of Spain. Walcott continued to publish poems and plays throughout the 1960s and his first collection of poetry, *Another Life* (1973), established him as a significant writer. Among more than 45 major works are the play *Dream on Monkey Mountain* (1970) and the 1990 epic *Omeros*, a broad narrative that mixes Homeric legend with West Indian themes. More recently, he collaborated with singer Paul Simon in the Broadway musical *The Capeman*.

Walcott's ethnic origins are British, Dutch and African; his culture French and British with an American twist; and his sensibility wholly West Indian. In awarding Walcott the prize, the Nobel academy commented that "In him, West Indian culture has found its great poet", and called his work "a poetic oeuvre of great luminosity, sustained by a historical vision, the outcome of a multicultural achievement". Today, Derek Walcott divides his time between homes in St Lucia and in the United States, where he is a professor of English at Boston University.

this small city centrepiece is a grassy, landscaped oasis in an otherwise congested town. Benches and resting spots are scattered around – favoured perches at lunchtime for local

DEREK WALCOTT SQUARE

office workers grabbing a quick bite in the shade. The east side of the square is shaded by an immense saman tree, thought to be more than 400 years old. Samans are also known as **rain trees** – their leaves so thick and plentiful that after a downpour, the tree continues to "rain". The small gazebo adjacent to the tree is used for band concerts and public gatherings. A **memorial** and plaque dedicated to native St Lucians who died during the world wars occupies the west end of the park.

BRAZIL STREET

Map 2, D6–F6.

Located on the south side of Derek Walcott Square, **Brazil Street** is the city's crowded and frenetic architectural showcase. Miraculously, many of its structures escaped the hurricanes and fires of the early colonial days and the mid-twentieth century and excellent examples of **colonial West Indian architecture** stand directly across from the square. The beautiful white Victorian town house with green trim festooned by white gingerbread fretwork dates back to 1885, and is one of the city's best-preserved structures. Next door are two equally ornate buildings of the same period and also sporting the gingerbread motif; they were once inhabited by French barons and members of the English aristocracy, depending on which country was colonizing the island at the time, and are now private residences and shops. A short stroll to the east is an elaborate structure with a second-storey verandah decked out with intricate fretwork.

For visitors with a particular interest in colonial architecture, the St Lucia National Trust (see p.132) organizes the **Castries Heritage Walk**, an informed stroll around all the city's main sights.

CATHEDRAL OF THE IMMACULATE CONCEPTION

Map 2, E6. Services Sat 7.30pm, Sun 6am & 7.30am, Children's Mass Sun 10.30am. Donations accepted. ☎452-2271.

Nearly ninety percent of St Lucians are **Roman Catholic** – a legacy of years of French colonial rule – and the cornerstone of the island's faith is the imposing brick-and-mortar **Cathedral of the Immaculate Conception** on Laborie and Micoud streets, which seats two thousand communicants. The cathedral site has been occupied by various churches as far back as the early eighteenth century, all of which were destroyed by successive fires and storms. The foundation of the current structure dates to 1894, but today's building was not completed until 1931. In 1957, the former church was granted the status of a cathedral, and was visited by **Pope John Paul II** when he toured the Caribbean in 1986.

Unless Mass is in progress, you're allowed inside to have a look around the ornate **interior**, bathed in rich red and diffused yellow light from ceiling portals, and busy with

MURDER IN THE CATHEDRAL

On December 31, 2000, several members of a local cult claiming to align itself with the Rastafarian faith barged into the cathedral with flaming torches and clubs, setting fire to the members of the congregation, fatally burning the priest officiating at the mass, and bludgeoning a nun to death. Rastafarians throughout the island condemned the attack, denying any link to their religion, and the men who were caught have not given the reasons behind their vicious act. There have been two further attempts at such antics made by the cult, but security is now greatly improved and both proved unsuccessful.

detailed carved wood inlay, wooden benches, iron ceiling supports and stately pillars. Note the remarkably colourful ceiling paintings of Catholic saints and apostles, with St Lucie in the centre, and the vivid wall murals, depicting black saints and the work of the Catholic Church in St Lucia painted before the visit of Pope John Paul II in 1985 by island artist **Dunstan St Omer**, who also designed St Lucia's flag.

CENTRAL MARKET TO LA PLACE CARENAGE

Map 2, D4–E4. Daily.

Exuberant, vividly colourful and often loud, the enclosed **Central Market** on Jeremie Street at the northern perimeter of downtown is one of the busiest parts of Castries and a must-see for visitors. This rambling, unplanned structure actually houses several markets, all of which are at their most frenetic on Saturday mornings. Inside are rows of **craft booths**, with vendors selling baskets, spices, carvings, T-shirts, straw hats and tacky souvenirs. The prices here are about as good as they get, and certainly better than at Pointe Seraphine (see p.66), but do tend to increase a little if a cruise ship is in town. In the centre of the craft section is a non-functioning cement **fountain** resplendent with protruding lion heads painted bright red; a sign above implores: "No Smoking, No Spitting". The fountain is the most obvious remnant of the original market, built in 1894; you can still see parts of the old iron structure in the ceiling and walls.

Under an orange roof to the left of the Jeremie Street entrance, the **fruit and vegetable market** offers a wealth of exotic fresh produce: mangoes, sugar cane, soursop, ginger, bananas, plantains and earth-encrusted tubers of yam and dasheen piled high on cardboard boxes or makeshift stands of wood. Prices here are lower and the quality much higher than anything you will find in the island's lacklustre supermarkets. Some vendors also put out their stalls in the open air at the back of the market.

Also at the market's back end, on the north side, an alley-way of fifteen or so small, steam- and smoke-belching **restaurant stalls** (see p.179) fill the air with tempting aromas. Inexpensive and reliable, these are possibly the best places to eat in town, serving up huge portions of seafood, rotis, rice and beans, or meat and dumpling dishes at plastic tables jammed into the narrow corridor between the stalls. At the end of the restaurant arcade, **Lewis Street** is also lined with shops and vendors selling vegetables, fruit and crafts.

Across from the Central Market on **Peynier Street**, and easily identifiable by the rust-coloured roof, is the **Vendor's Arcade**, another set of craft stalls selling the same rather tacky wares at slightly higher prices.

Heading west from the Central Market along Jeremie Street, with the harbour on your right, **La Place Carenage** duty-free shopping centre is five minutes' walk away. Though not as large as the mall at Pointe Seraphine, the centre has several craft and vegetable stalls, art galleries and boutiques. You'll find some good deals here, without the trouble of travelling over the water to Pointe Seraphine. La Place Carenage shops are generally open weekdays from 9am to 4pm, Saturday from 9am to 1pm, and, if cruise ships are visiting, some are also open on Sunday from 9am to 4pm. You'll need both your passport and your airline ticket if you plan to take advantage of the duty-free prices here.

Vigie Peninsula

Framing the northern half of Port Castries, and a short drive or five-minute water taxi ride away from downtown, the heavily developed **Vigie Peninsula** is partially made up of land recovered from the sea by successive government reclamation projects. At the south of the peninsula, and overlooking the bay, are the **Pointe Seraphine shopping complex** and two **cruise ship berths**, while government offices converted from eighteenth- and nineteenth-century military buildings are clustered around the sparsely developed western tip; a lighthouse overlooks the ocean here, but it's not open to visitors. Running almost diagonally through the centre of the peninsula is the George F.L. Charles Airport, and parallel to the runway is the expansive **Vigie Beach**, where there's a waterfront hotel and several excellent seafood restaurants.

POINTE SERAPHINE

Map 2, B2. Mon–Fri 9am–5pm, Sat 9am–2pm.

Outside the usual Caribbean tourist paraphernalia and comestibles, Castries is not a shopper's paradise. However, at the north end of the inner harbour, a small centre of consumerism exists in the form of the **Pointe Seraphine** duty-free complex. Built in the early 1990s on reclaimed land, Pointe Seraphine advertises itself as the Caribbean's biggest duty-free shopping complex. It's not (the honour goes to the Charlotte Amalie mall in the US Virgin Islands), but it is certainly the largest that St Lucia has to offer, and it's still growing. The two adjacent cruise ship berths deliver disembarking tourists directly to the stores, while the **taxi stand** (℡452-1733) and the **water taxi** to downtown Castries (see p.32) stand by to cater for the day trippers.

For more on shopping, see p.45.

The twenty-plus **shops** include international chain stores, as well as local retailers dealing in leather goods, cigars, music, souvenirs and art. You'll also find a branch of the National Commercial Bank and the *Sunshine Bookshop* here – the latter stocks a selection of British and US newspapers, including *The Times*, *Miami Herald* and the *New York Times*, usually a day or two old, as well as local papers. There are a number of bars and restaurants but none are particularly recommendable.

ALONG PENINSULAR ROAD

Map 3, A5–D5.

Sandwiched between the airport runway and the sea, **Peninsular Road** runs east to west along the length of Vigie Peninsula. To get on to it, take the John Compton Highway north from downtown, turn right on the Castries-Gros Islet Highway, left at the end of the airport and left again onto the Peninsular Road. Just before you reach the airstrip, the **Choc Cemetery** is on the right, typical of those in the region with its ornately decorated raised white tombs. Forty simple white memorial stones standing in sentry around a large white cross designate the **War Cemetery** section, dedicated to local sailors who were killed in March 1942, when a German submarine skulked into Castries harbour and torpedoed two British ships.

Just west of the cemetery, Peninsular Road flanks the two-kilometre **Vigie Beach**; long and smooth, but with litter-strewn, brown-grey sand, it's not much to look at, but the water is usually calm and inviting. A few snack vendors are parked here and there, a handful of benches and picnic tables overlook the water, and there's plenty of shade from trees, but for better places to swim and sun yourself, head north to Reduit (see p.86) or south toward Marigot (see p.98).

Once clear of the airport, Peninsular Road winds uphill towards its apex at Vigie Lighthouse. The entire peninsula was once a fortification, and many of the buildings at the top of the hill are restored military quarters, built from red brick in the late nineteenth century. At the western end of the peninsula, St Lucia's **National Archives** (Mon–Thurs 9am–4pm, Fri 9am–2pm; ☎452-1654) are housed in a circa-1890 building: inside, you can browse through hundreds of old photos, lithographs, postcards and maps, which provide a good historical perspective of the island. Ensconced in an ex-military building adjacent to the archives are the offices of the **St Lucia National Trust** (Mon–Fri 8.30am–4.30pm; ☎452-5005, Ⓦwww.slunatrust .org), where you can obtain brochures and information pamphlets about nature reserves such as the Fregate and Maria islands. A society that seeks to preserve historical sites and other places of national interest, the National Trust has proposed that the entire peninsula be designated a protected site, with the island's first national museum located among the barracks; however, the plans are unlikely to be realized in the foreseeable future.

North and east of Castries

Past the Vigie Peninsula, **Choc Bay**'s enviable stretch of golden sand and lively beach bars make a great place to get away from the city heat; just offshore, tiny **Rat Island** has long shrugged off its former role as a quarantine station and has been earmarked by Nobel Prize-winner Derek Walcott as a possible site for an artists' colony. Inland from Choc Bay, a smooth, wide road heads toward **Babonneau**, a typical inland village which was home to several vast sugar plantations during the eighteenth century. Also in the interior but to the northeast of downtown Castries, the **Folk Research Centre** provides a fascinating and unique insight into St Lucian traditions.

CHOC BAY

Map 1, E3.

Heading north from Castries, the busy Castries–Gros Islet Highway passes the Vigie Peninsula to the left, through a string of industrial sites, shops, restaurants, hotels and schools. It's not the most appealing drive on the island, but five minutes out of town and past the peninsula, the highway runs parallel to the two-kilometre sweep of **Choc Bay**, fringed to the north by Labrellotte Point, a compact, sheltered bay hosting a couple of luxury resorts, and to the south by **Vide Bouteille Point**, a small promontory which separates Choc and Vigie bays and was the site of St Lucia's first **fort**, built in 1660 by the French – there's nothing left of it today.

From the highway, you'll catch tempting glimpses of the hidden **coves** and honey-coloured sand **beaches** that

RAT ISLAND

A diminutive cay scattered with scrubby trees and dilapidated buildings, Rat Island (Map 3, E3) lies a few hundred yards off the coast at the southern end of Choc Bay. Though currently uninhabited, the island has been occupied in the past – periodic finds of Arawak pottery suggest that Amerindians once settled here, and the cay was also put to use as a quarantine station for afflictions such as scarlet fever and smallpox, before being abandoned in the late nineteenth century when infection levels fell.

Rat Island is notable today for its connection with St Lucia's Nobel Prize-winner Derek Walcott (see box on p.61), who, in conjunction with the government of St Lucia, private donors and grants from Boston University – known collectively as the Rat Island Foundation – has proposed the island be redeveloped as an artists' retreat so that its "extraordinary solitude" can be fully utilized. The not-yet-formal plans include several cottages, as well as a dock, jetty and an amphitheatre intended to attract artists, writers and actors from St Lucia and further afield. For now the island cannot be visited, and no tours stop here.

pepper Choc Bay, some lined by hotels. The beaches are accessible via several turnoffs, but one of the best places to spend a day is the stretch adjacent to *The Wharf*, a lively beach bar and restaurant with good food, a nightly 5–6pm happy hour and an affiliated watersports concession. Equally pleasant is the stretch of Vigie Beach in front of *D's Restaurant*, where you can grab some lunch before heading to the water.

Reviews of accommodation around Castries start on p.155; for eating and drinking listings, see p.180.

CHOC BAY

BABONNEAU

Map 1, F4.

About 3km north of the capital at the southern end of Choc Bay, the Castries–Gros Islet Highway swings into the suburban Sunny Acres area. On the inland side of the road is **Gablewoods Mall**, one of the island's larger shopping complexes and the best place to go if you need to visit a pharmacy or buy groceries. Just past the mall, the winding **Allan Bousquet Highway** strikes into the interior – ten minutes' drive eastward from the coast is the village of **BABONNEAU**, a small farming community huddled in the central hills of the island's northern half, and worth visiting for the sweeping views and a taste of rural St Lucia. Several rivers flow through the hills around the settlement and some people believe that the town's name is a Patois version of the old French phrase *barre bon eau*, meaning, roughly, "mountain ridge, good water".

The Allan Bousquet Highway is the easiest route
to the attractions of the northeast coast, including
the turtle watch at Grande Anse beach (see p.136).

Babonneau was settled early on in St Lucia's history by Joseph Tascher de la Pagerie, who owned an estate at nearby Paix Bouche and fathered Marie-Joseph Tascher de la Pagerie, better known as **Empress Josephine** of France, wife of Napoleon Bonaparte (see box overleaf). However, despite the historical infamy, there's not a great deal to see in Babonneau other than a large and brightly coloured **Catholic church** on a hill in the sparsely populated "centre" of the village, which dates back to 1947.

BABONNEAU

EMPRESS JOSEPHINE

St Lucians popularly believe that the girl who would become Empress Josephine, wife of Napoleon Bonaparte, came into the world at a plantation estate called Paix Bouche, near Babonneau. However, many in neighbouring Martinique claim that she was born on their island, and Josephine's birth records remain a hotly disputed matter of St Lucian national pride. As no birth certificate exists, and the various claims have been supported only by the memories of priests ministering in the late eighteenth century, proof is more a matter of legend than fact. St Lucians will grudgingly acknowledge that Josephine was conceived in Martinique, born in St Lucia and lived here for seven years, before returning to Martinique with her family.

Born Marie-Joseph Tascher de la Pagerie in 1763, Josephine was the daughter of estate owner Joseph Tascher de la Pagerie. In 1779, at the age of 16, she married French military officer and nobleman Alexandre, Vicomte de Beauharnais. Due to his status as a nobleman, Beauharnais was one of many singled out during the French Revolution's reign of terror, and was beheaded in 1794. Josephine married Napoleon in 1796, and became empress when the megalomaniacal leader declared himself emperor in 1804. The marriage was short-lived – Napoleon divorced her in 1809, and she died in 1814. Josephine had two children with Beauharnais, Eugène and Hortense. Keeping things in the family, Hortense later married Napoleon's brother Louis and bore him a son, the future empire leader Napoleon III.

A few kilometres further inland from Babonneau is the Union Nature Trail centre – an agricultural station, mini zoo and hiking trail (see p.142).

FOLK RESEARCH CENTRE

Map 3, D6. Mon–Fri 8.30am–4.30pm. Donations accepted. Morne Pleasant. Ⓣ453-1477.

Set high in the hills east of Castries at Morne Pleasant, the **Folk Research Centre** (or *Plas Wichès Foklò*, to give it its Patois name) is a museum and cultural centre set in an old estate house originally owned by the eminent Deveaux family. The small **museum** consists of a somewhat jumbled but interesting display of cultural artefacts, including a reproduction of a traditional *ti-kay* hut and examples of indigenous musical instruments such as the *chak chak* (condiment tins taped together and filled with seeds), *banjo bwa payé* (a small banjo) and *tambou* (a wooden drum with a goatskin head). Also on display are clay pots and a diorama depicting an ancient St Lucian legend of a witch doctor stepping through a magic door. The small **research library** upstairs holds one of the island's best collections of books, research papers and photographs relating to St Lucia's folklore and history. You can view the collection during opening hours and librarians are on hand to assist you.

Since it was established in 1973, the centre has spearheaded the movement to preserve and promote St Lucia's heritage and St Lucian Creole, and is especially active during **Carnival**. During the festival, you can call in for a schedule of plays, musical performances and special events based around the celebrations, which take place here and throughout the island. The centre is also the focal point of International Creole Day, or *Jounen Kwéyòl*, and runs a programme of lectures within local schools, as well as staging performances by the in-house **Popular Theatre** group, also known by their Patois name *Tèyat Pep La*; for more on their productions, see p.200.

For more on St Lucia's Carnival, see p.199.

To get to the centre, turn off the Castries–Gros Islet Highway along the L'Anse Road, which heads inland just south of the airport; you turn off again at the sign for Morne Pleasant.

South and west of Castries

Though the capital provides tempting views of far-flung peaks such as the Pitons at Soufrière (see p.112) and of Morne Gimie in the southern interior, the hills that surround the capital allow you to take in the city and much of the north coast; on clear days you can see the island of Martinique, some 40km to the north. West of town the British-built **La Toc Battery** is one of the island's best-preserved stockades, while the historically significant **Morne Fortune** hills to the south are riddled with remnants of French forts dating back to the eighteenth and nineteenth centuries. Snaking through Morne Fortune's southern foothills, the coastal highway swings down into the verdant and beautiful **Cul de Sac Valley**, noted for its extensive banana fields and for the jarringly unpleasant Hess Oil plant.

LA TOC BATTERY

Map 3, A7. Dec–April daily 9am–3pm. May–Nov by appointment only. EC$6. ☎451-6300.

From downtown Castries, La Toc Road leads west along the south side of the harbour. Toward the western outskirts of town, as the road begins to climb, is the sizeable Victoria Hospital, the island's largest; a mile or so beyond, still on La Toc Road, is **La Toc Battery**, one of the island's best-preserved examples of British military bastions. This 2.5-acre, nineteenth-century cement fortification features mounted cannons and dim underground bunkers, tunnels and cartridge storage rooms; one of the bunkers holds a large exhibit of antique bottles. If military history doesn't interest you, the superb views down to the southern entrance to Castries harbour almost certainly will, and there's also a small **botanical garden** where guides conduct tours at no extra cost.

MORNE FORTUNE

Map 3, B8–C8.

In order to pass from Castries to the south of the island you have to wind through the loosely demarcated suburb of **Morne Fortune** (also known as "The Morne"). Comprising a series of hills which flank the capital to the south, the area's high elevation provides striking views of the city, the Vigie Peninsula and the north coast – on a clear day you can see Martinique – and to the south, glimpses of the conical Pitons at Soufrière. The area is reached via Manoel Street in downtown Castries, which becomes Government House Road as it begins its snakelike ascent.

The main historic attraction of the Morne Fortune hills are the eighteenth- and nineteenth-century military installations of **Fort Charlotte**, most still standing and now forming part of an educational and government administrative complex. Parts of the old fort complex are open to the public, while others await restoration.

Also scattered throughout The Morne are several excellent **restaurants**, great places for lunch with panoramic views of the harbour below. While you're in the area, its also well worth checking out **Eudovic Art Studio, Guest House and Restaurant** (T452-2747; Wwww.stluciatravel .com.lc/eudovic.htm) on the southern flanks of the hills, where you can watch local **wood carvers** create some extraordinary works under the watchful eye of master artisan Vincent Joseph Eudovic. One of the island's most renowned carvers, Eudovic studied in Africa and works in mahogany, teak and cedar to produce abstract, graceful and flowing pieces. He also uses the local wood laurier canelle, now thought to be extinct, but found as stumps and buried roots in the rainforests. The restaurant here is decent enough, and the guesthouse rooms are pleasant and have garden views (**2**).

Government House

Map 3, B7. Open by appointment only Tues & Thurs 10am–noon and 2pm–4pm. T452-2481.

Unsurprisingly, the focal point of Government House Road, and just south of downtown Castries, is the official residence of the governor general, **Government House**, an imposing, white Victorian two-storey structure dating from 1895 and visible from Castries. The building houses the small **Le Pavillon Royal Museum** (Tues & Thurs 10am–noon & 2pm–4pm, by appointment only; Wwww .lepavillonroyal.com), where you can see a large if somewhat dull collection of artefacts and documents relating to the history of the house, photographs and documents pertaining to past prime ministers and significant modern St Lucian artefacts. A **viewing platform** set just below the building affords wonderful views of Castries below.

Fort Charlotte

Map 3, B8.

A few winds and turns beyond Government House, Morne
Road takes you into the heart of Morne Fortune and to the
top of the 260-metre Morne Fortune itself, named "Good
Luck Hill" by the French. The hills were first fortified by the
French in 1768, then recaptured (and renamed **Fort
Charlotte**) by the British in 1803. A great **battle** was fought
here in 1796 – a monument on the grounds of Sir Arthur
Lewis College (see box on p.77) honours the victorious
Royal Inniskilling Fusiliers, who fought for several days on
the steep slopes to take the position from the French.

Several of the existing military encampments, cemeteries,
barracks and batteries are slated to be restored and opened
to the public; however, the process is incomplete and many
are still in a state of disrepair. Among those that have
received some attention is the **Apostles' Battery**, just off
the road south of Government House. Built in 1888–90, it's
so named for its four mounted ten-inch guns, but the
expansive views from here are probably more eyecatching
than the ruin itself. Back on the road and a few hundred
metres to the east is **Provost's Redout**, another gun battery built in 1782, also with gorgeous views to the northwest coast. Other sites, not yet refurbished, include the
nineteenth-century Old English Cemetery, the old prison
cells, guard room and stables.

The best-preserved remnants of the fort are now part of a
multipurpose government complex that encompasses offices
of the Agricultural Department, the Caribbean
Environmental Health Institute and the Organization of
Eastern Caribbean States, as well as the **Sir Arthur Lewis
Community College**, named after the St Lucian Nobel
Prize-winner (see box on p.78), who is buried in a private
plot in the grounds. The college itself comprises several

MORNE FORTUNE

SIR ARTHUR LEWIS

Of the three Nobel laureates born on West Indian soil, St Lucia has the honour of claiming two as expatriate sons: Derek Walcott, winner of the literature prize in 1992 (see box on p.61), and the economist Sir Arthur Lewis, technically a Lucian adoptee, who was actually born on Antigua in 1915, but emigrated to St Lucia with his family at the age of 3. After completing his secondary education at 14, he won a scholarship to study in England. Lewis originally intended to study engineering, but gave up the idea when he realized that, given the tenor of the times, firms were not hiring black engineers. He eventually studied commerce and accounting at the London School of Economics and went on to earn a PhD in Industrial Economics.

Lewis became a professor of economics at the University of Manchester in England, and, in 1963, the year he was knighted for extraordinary service to the realm, he earned a full professorship at Princeton University in New Jersey. Lewis's 1954 book *The Theory of Economic Growth* is still regarded as a seminal work in the field of world economic history, and he was also an economic advisor to the United Nations and played an important role in establishing the Caribbean Development Bank in the early 1970s. Shared with American Theodore Schultz, Lewis's Nobel Prize for Economics came in 1979. He died in 1991 aged 76.

larger, nineteenth-century yellow-brick structures with gleaming white columns, all of military origin, which include the Combermere Barracks, a series of three buildings named after Lord Combermere, the commander of British forces in St Lucia between 1817 and 1820. Featuring thick walls, second-floor balconies and archways framing entrance portals, the college's buildings were restored in the late 1960s and look surprisingly modern due to careful refurbishment and ongoing upkeep. You're free to amble about and visit the buildings and Inniskilling monument, which is on the south side of the college complex behind the Combermere Barracks.

CUL DE SAC VALLEY

Map 1, D5.

As you head south over the Morne Fortune hills, the immense **Cul de Sac Valley** swings into view as the Castries–Soufrière highway begins to descend. Chiselled out by the Cul de Sac River, one of the island's longest, the valley's relatively flat and extremely fertile plains make it ideal for **farming**, and the area is abundant with banana fields and small holdings. The only blight on the land is the large, modern **Hess Oil plant** and its massive shipping docks, as well as the large main plant of the island's electricity company, Lucelec. Just past Lucelec is the eastbound turnoff for Dennery and the Department of Forest and Lands' Barre de L'Isle Trail (see p.143). The road to Dennery is in great shape, and you can get to the east coast town in twenty minutes or so (see p.133).

South of the valley, the main road heads toward Marigot Bay and, ultimately, Soufrière and the south coast.

Gros Islet and the north

In accordance with French administrative divisions that split the island into eleven quartiers, St Lucia's compact northern tip is still referred to as the Quarter of Gros Islet. The area encompasses the "Golden Mile" resort towns of the northwest coast as well as the remote and arid northern shoreline between Pointe du Cap and Pointe Hardy, and quiet Cas-en-Bas on the rugged northeast coast.

On the west coast, the sweeping, three-kilometre horseshoe of Rodney Bay contains the majority of the Quarter's tourist trappings. **Rodney Bay** town is the most popular resort area, with a deep-water yacht harbour and a sophisticated marina complex packed with shops and restaurants, as well as the superlative, hotel-lined **Reduit Beach**, one of St Lucia's most popular strips of sand with excellent watersports. You'd be forgiven for thinking that the accommodation here would be limited to flashy resorts, but in fact this strip offers a smorgasbord of hotels, villas, guesthouses and eateries for all budgets and tastes. Across the harbour channel is the usually quiet fishing village of **Gros Islet**, a place to soak up some local flavour. Every Friday night just about the entire town is overtaken for the raucous street party – the famous "**jump-up**". Gros Islet's beach isn't one of the northwest's best, but on the opposite coastline, **Cas-en-Bas** boasts several secluded places to swim.

Rodney Bay's northern half is framed by **Pigeon Island National Historic Park**. Heavily fortified by the British in the eighteenth century, the "island" has been transformed into a recreation park that is home to the restored remains of military buildings, a string of beaches and walking trails. The park also showcases concerts of the **St Lucia Jazz Festival** (see p.198).

Despite all the development along the northwest coast, the north does not feel particularly crowded. Many of the lodgings are secreted away along the shoreline itself, and though the Castries–Gros Islet Highway is thick with vehicles on the outskirts of the capital, both the traffic and the tourist buzz thin out north of Pigeon Island, as the road meanders toward hilly **Cap Estate**. Here, the Quarter takes on a more natural and rugged feel: calm Caribbean coastline is replaced by cliffs and choppy waters, and the parched peaks provide marvellous views of both the northern coast and the island of Martinique. A couple of exclusive resorts occupy the coast, while the eastern hills around **Saline Point** and **Pointe du Cap** (St Lucia's most northerly extremity) are scattered with the palatial homes and villas of the island's elite. The rough roads to the east coast from Saline Point pass the hardy vegetation of cacti and acacia that indicate the aridity of the region. Rarely visited by tourists, **Pointe Hardy** juts out into the Atlantic at the island's northeast tip, and provides stunning panoramas of the rocky coast, cliffs and crashing surf.

Some history

Artefacts have been found both around Gros Islet and on Pigeon Island, evidence of Carib – and possibly Arawak – settlement dating back 1500 years. However, the earliest written reference to the area is contained in a French map of 1717, which labelled the spot "Le Gros Islet" or "Large Island" for the offshore cay now known as Pigeon Island. This small spit of land gained further notability in 1782, when Britain's Admiral George Rodney established a **fort** there, which he used as a base to engage the French (see p.89). Like most other St Lucian settlements fought for by both Britain and France, the area soon had two names, earning its French title of La Revolution less than ten years after it had become Fort Rodney. When the British regained control of St Lucia later in the century, the name reverted to Gros Islet, and surrounding sugar plantations such as Bonne Terre and Marisule provided some prosperity.

For more on St Lucia's history, see p.225.

At the turn of the twentieth century, Gros Islet itself was little more than a bucolic fishing village bordered by a great marsh. However, during World War II, Allied forces constructed **naval airfields** at Gros Islet (and at Vieux Fort) for the defence of the Panama Canal and the interests of the United States against the German U-boats and other vessels of war that skulked in the area. The naval engineers' attempts to fill in the large mangrove swamp south of the village met, time after time, with failure. At the end of the war, the bases were dismantled and gradually crumbled, but the idea of creating an **inner harbour** to the naturally deep Rodney Bay had taken hold. In 1970, the government dredged the mangrove swamp and let it fill – the ensuing harbour is now home to one of the island's largest marinas

– using sand and sludge removed from the swamp to construct the Pigeon Island causeway.

Inevitably, though, damage has been done. The swamp was once a prime breeding and feeding area for hundreds of species of migrating birds and marine life, such as cattle egrets, herons, the St Lucia black finch and oriole as well as prawns, spiny lobster and conch, most of which have now moved elsewhere. The jury remains out regarding the deeper **environmental issues** – the natural filtration systems provided by the swamp are gone, and ocean currents that flowed around Pigeon Island have been interrupted by the causeway. Some reports indicate increased pollution of the waters immediately offshore, but at the moment, there seems little to dampen the northwest's appeal.

Getting there and around

Getting to and around St Lucia's northern end is relatively easy, since frequent **buses** run the length of the coast between Castries, Gros Islet and Cap Estate. Marked Route 1a, they leave from Castries from the Marketing Board behind the Central Market on Jeremie Street. Schedules are academic as buses tend to leave when they are full or ready, but count on at least one departure every hour from 6.30am until 10pm, with more services for the jump-up on Friday night. You'll pay EC$2.50 to travel from Castries to Reduit Beach, Rodney Bay Marina or Gros Islet. If you're travelling from farther afield, you'll have to change buses at Castries. If you don't have a car and would rather avoid public transport, the most hassle-free mode of transport is to hire a **taxi**. From downtown Castries to any of the resorts along the northeast coast, expect to pay around EC$40–50.

It's not as easy to get around the island's extreme northern tip, or from the northeast coast across to the northwest coast. Though it's just a few kilometres from one coastline to the other, travelling over the dirt roads that traverse this section of the Quarter – which includes Pointe Hardy, Pointe du Cap and Saline Point – is not an easy proposition, particularly after rain, when a 4WD is recommended.

RODNEY BAY AND REDUIT BEACH

Map 4, E7–F7.

Named **RODNEY BAY** after eighteenth-century British Admiral George Brydges Rodney (see box opposite), the current incarnation of this former American army base is a compact but fully fledged tourist resort, sandwiched between the glorious **Reduit Beach** and the shops and yachting facilities of **Rodney Bay Marina**. The mangrove swamp that once separated the villages of Rodney Bay and Gros Islet (see p.86) has been replaced by a man-made harbour channel cutting between the two settlements, which opens out into a deep-water lagoon dotted with bobbing yachts. From the Castries–Gros Islet Highway, the main road into town is on the left side, immediately before the unmissable JQ's shopping mall and just south of the harbour and marina; if you can see the marina on the left, you've gone too far.

The settlement itself is quite small, and as most of its few roads lead to the beach, you'll find that it's difficult to get lost. Most of the activity is split between the beach and the Rodney Bay Marina – widely accepted as one of the finest marinas in the Caribbean, with plenty of slips and full services for boaters. Unfortunately, the marina's restaurants and gift shops have become a bit disappointing in recent years – for a decent meal and a holiday atmosphere, you'd be better off heading to Reduit Beach. The complex is a good spot for booking **watersports**: numerous operators are based here, with activities ranging from scuba diving, deep-

ADMIRAL GEORGE RODNEY

Admiral George Brydges Rodney (1718–92) looms large in the history of the West Indies, particularly in the bloody French–British conflict over possession of key islands. Rodney entered the British navy in 1732 (at the age of 14) and distinguished himself in his late 20s by leading forces in British naval victories in Martinique – by 1778, he had become an admiral.

By 1782, Rodney had established part of his naval force at the Gros Islet harbour, today's Rodney Bay. From military observation points at Pigeon Island he was able to scrutinize French activity off the coast of northern Martinique. In April of that year the French fleet, under Admiral François de Grasse, sailed from Martinique, intending to join forces with their Spanish allies at Cap François, Haiti, and thereafter sail for Jamaica to attack Fort Charles, one of the largest British strongholds in the West Indies. Rodney countered by sailing his fleet to the Dominica Passage, between Guadeloupe and Dominica, where he cut off and engaged de Grasse's force. A fierce three-day battle ensued, known as the **Battle of the Saints** after the Guadeloupean Iles des Saintes archipelago. The British were victorious; de Grasse and seven French vessels were captured, effectively breaking the back of the French effort in the Caribbean, and winning Rodney the title of baron, bestowed on him by King George III of England.

sea fishing and pleasure boat cruises, to windboard, sailboat, car and motor craft rentals. At the south end of the marina, just after you turn into Rodney Bay from the highway, you can hop on a rather touristy **ferry to Pigeon Island** (℡452-8816; US$10). As taxis and buses will transport you for a fraction of the cost, the ferry is more a fun ride on the water than a necessity. From their booth next to *The Lime* restaurant in town, the Rodney Bay Ferry (℡452-0087) also offers straight transfers to Pigeon Island for US$10 or day-long picnic trips there for about US$45.

For details of accommodation in Rodney Bay and Gros Islet, see pp.160–164; for eating and drinking, see pp.183–187.

West of the marina lies the original reason for Rodney Bay's growth into a tourism epicentre: the inviting, easily accessible **Reduit Beach**, about 1km long and among the prettiest on the island, with a wide swath of fine white sand, generally calm surf, a few boats moored out in the bay and views of Pigeon Island to the north and the coastal hills to the south. However, this is no Caribbean haven: the beach is generally packed with the well-oiled bodies of the area's visiting sun worshippers and is not exactly a secluded hideaway. Unsurprisingly, it's also lined with places to stay, many of them large-scale but low-lying concrete blocks sitting directly, and intrusively, on the beach, and their proximity adds to the generally crowded feel. The beach hotels provide chairs and umbrellas for their guests and many will rent them out to visitors staying elsewhere for a daily rate of around US$10. There are also several **bars** and **restaurants** dotted along the shore, as well as some of the island's more celebrated entertainment spots and **clubs**, most of which are concentrated in a small area at the south end of the beach (see p.183).

GROS ISLET

Map 4, E6.

Located just across the channel from Rodney Bay, **Gros Islet** is a small, unprepossessing fishing village of rickety, rust-roofed wooden homes and narrow streets filled with fruit and vegetable vendors. The beach is somewhat dirty

FRIDAY NIGHT JUMP-UP

Come Friday night, Lucians and visitors alike pour in for Gros Islet's famous **street party** or **jump-up**, when everyone lets loose and parties. Much of the town is blocked off to traffic, and armies of snack vendors peddling barbecue, fried fish, hot cakes and cold beers arrive to cater to the hungry masses. Bars throw open their doors, speakers are set up on street corners and loud music is pumped out as the crowd gyrates to thumping soca and reggae. Things get going around 10pm and last till the wee hours of the morning, and, despite the distinctly sexual undertones, it's generally a good-natured affair consisting mainly of moving between vendors and dancing as best you can with a beer in one hand and a juicy barbecued chicken leg in the other. Be warned though, that, while there is an unobtrusive police presence, a slightly seedy side has developed recently. There will inevitably be several drunks, hustlers and hasslers in the crowd, including those selling illegal substances. Women – who really shouldn't attend alone – should be prepared for unwarranted attention; consider hiring a taxi driver as your guide. Common sense applies: leave your valuables at your hotel and refuse anything that seems suspect.

Some hotels will bus guests to the party, but it's better to arrange for a taxi driver to pick you up at a specified time or you'll have to rely on the rather sketchy bus schedule.

and generally the town holds little of interest for the visitor, except the boisterous Friday night **jump-up** (see box above).

Though there is little to distinguish Gros Islet in terms of architectural merit, one building worth a look is the imposing **St Joseph the Worker Roman Catholic Church** on Church Street, a block north of Dauphine Street, the main drag. It's an ornate structure with a cement facade, built in 1926 on the site of a church destroyed by a 1906 earthquake. There's also a **public library** on Marie Theresa Street across from *Daphil's Hotel* (see p.163).

Dotted with fishing boats, drying nets and small vendor huts as well as some unappealing detritus, the thin public **beach** along **Bay Street** is generally quiet, and passable for swimming – for better beaches, however, make the short trip to Reduit Beach at Rodney Bay, or the causeway beach at Pigeon Island on the north side of Gros Islet. If you want to **stay** in Gros Islet, there are several guesthouses along Marie Therese and Bay streets (see p.163), while the local restaurants scattered around town are basic but offer authentic, satisfying Creole fare (see p.187).

CAS-EN-BAS AND AROUND

Map 1, F1.

Just past Gros Islet at the Shell petrol station, a dirt track known as the Cas-en-Bas Road strikes east off the coastal highway toward a small settlement on the remote east coast called **CAS-EN-BAS**, worth visiting for its string of secluded **beaches**. You can walk the track in an hour, much more appealing than negotiating the endless mucky potholes by 4WD – don't even attempt it after rain, or in a regular car. Alternatively, you could approach the beaches via the road behind the golf course in Cap Estate, a much less exhausting, albeit less interesting, option.

The Cas-en-Bas road ends at the ocean, where you'll find a wonderful, quiet beach with some shady spots and an outlying reef taming the rougher waters of the Atlantic. There's an even more isolated spot, **Secret Beach**, ten minutes' walk north, along a trail that hugs the rocky, cactus-strewn coastline – look out for a track that goes back down to the water. A few more minutes north along the coastal track brings you past an open field to another seapath, along which, after half an hour or so, you'll find a remote spot of honey-coloured sand known as **Donkey Beach**.

Visitors to the shores of Cas-en-Bas should take the utmost care in the water here, for these unmarked and unmanned beaches have seen many people – locals and tourists alike – drown, victims of powerful Atlantic **undercurrents**. The area is deserted, so tell someone where you are going before you set off.

Thirty minutes' walk **south** of Cas-en-Bas along the unmarked coastal path brings you to the beach at **Anse Lavoutte**, favoured by **leatherback turtles** as a secluded spot for egg-laying between March and July. If you want to witness this spectacle for yourself, you must join a turtle watch (see p.136).

PIGEON ISLAND NATIONAL HISTORIC PARK

Map 1, E1. Daily 9am–5pm. EC$10 or US$4; EC$30 for a 10-day pass; children under 12 EC$1.

Back on the west coast, the 45-acre **PIGEON ISLAND NATIONAL HISTORIC PARK** is a handsome promontory of land striking into the ocean just north of Gros Islet. Contrary to its name, it ceased being an island in the 1970s when it was linked to the mainland via a causeway. Today, it's one of St Lucia's most popular relaxation spots, a combination of historic site, hiking trails, concert venue and pleasant stop for lunch with the added bonus of several excellent beaches and a fine pub. In the hotter months, you'd be wise to visit early in the day as you may want to explore the island's excellent hill views – a much more pleasant experience before the sun becomes unbearably strong.

History of the park

The island has a chequered **history** and has served as a base for several notable inhabitants, from the Arawaks, who are alleged to have left behind clay pottery, to the infamous pirate François Leclerc, also known as Jambe de Bois or Wooden Leg (see box below). In 1778, Pigeon Island was fortified by the newly arrived British colonists, and it was from here that Admiral Rodney (see box on p.85) launched the attack against the French that effectively ended their domination of the Caribbean. When African slaves were given their freedom by French Republicans following the French Revolution, imminent British repossession of the island combined with fear of re-enslavement spurred them into action. Tagged as the "**Brigands**", the Africans banded together to create a minor rebellion of their own, razing plantations and even taking brief possession of the heavily

FRANÇOIS LECLERC

One of Pigeon Island's more colourful past inhabitants was François Leclerc, a French sea captain turned freebooter nicknamed Jambe de Bois for his suitably piratical **wooden leg** (there's no record of how his limb was lost). Leclerc arrived in the Caribbean sometime around 1550, and used Pigeon Island as a strategic, protected hideout and base for five years. He is believed to have pulled off some sort of truce with the habitually aggressive Caribs, and is known to have captured at least four cargo ships in his time; survivors of these sea battles were either killed or invited to join his buccaneer crew. He often sank the barren hulks of the ships he stripped for supplies, and legend has it that he secreted **treasure** somewhere along the northern shore of the island, near Pigeon Point. He moved on sometime after 1554, but no records exist of his fate.

fortified Pigeon Island before signing a peace treaty in 1798. Following that period, the cay served variously as a camp for indentured East Indian labourers and a quarantine station for patients afflicted with the tropical disease known as yaws, and had a brief incarnation as a whaling station between 1909 and 1925.

In the 1970s, the entire 45 acres were designated a national landmark and afforded the protection of the St Lucia National Trust. The buildings were restored, the causeway was constructed, and Britain's Princess Alexandra opened the park to the public on February 23, 1979, the day St Lucia gained its independence.

Visiting the park

If you turn west from the Castries–Gros Islet Highway along the causeway, at the exit signposted for the complex, the first part of the park that you'll pass is a long and wide public **beach**, set opposite the village of Gros Islet and forming the northern fringe of Rodney Bay. At around 1km long, it's one of St Lucia's longer shorelines, and one of the calmest – you'll rarely encounter rolling surf. **Snorkelling** is decent along the main stretch, and if you follow the beach toward the main part of the park, there are several more good, though rocky, spots to don mask and flippers. This long swath of sand is popular with St Lucians on weekends, so expect some crowds, but there is plenty of space for parking, some shaded areas to sit and vendors selling cold drinks, fruit and barbecued food. The causeway leading to Pigeon Island is not quite as scenic as it once was, unfortunately, due mainly to the construction of a large resort hotel, complete with garishly bright blue roof, which has drastically altered the aesthetics of this once wide-open seashore.

Once you've passed the main gate at Pigeon Island, paid

your entrance fee and collected a free map (there's also a large and informative map on a sign board just past the entrance), the **Pigeon Island Museum and Interpretive Centre** is on your right, just past the crumbling ruins of the old officers' kitchen and itself located in the old officers' mess. A mini-museum of the island's past, the one-room centre is worth a brief look, and has displays of Amerindian axes, clay bowls, flint and shell tools and antique colonial furniture; a twenty-minute video presentation describing the history of St Lucia in a nutshell is available. The centre's gift shop sells history pamphlets and books, souvenirs and locally produced rum. Just below the centre is the wonderfully cavernous **Captain's Cellar Pub** (see p.187), a bar housed in the old barracks where you can head for an ice-cold pint of Piton after tackling the island's hills.

Past the Interpretive Centre, the south side of the island is peppered with the remains of the **military barracks** and **encampments** built by the British, including gun batteries, a powder magazine, a lime kiln and what's left of **Fort Rodney** (see p.82). As most of these ruins comprise crumbling brick walls with no roofs, or steps leading to foundations devoid of buildings, you'll need a little imagination to visualize just how well fortified a bastion Pigeon Island must have been. Some structures are more intact than others, such as the thick-walled powder magazine to the left of the entrance and the old cooperage near the beach on the south side of the island, which now houses toilet facilities. You can explore the ruins via the marked **walking trails** that traverse most of the island, but some of the decaying structures have signs warning visitors off. Every May, impromptu stages are set up in the open spaces among the ruins to host **St Lucia Jazz Festival** concerts; folk performances, local comedy shows featuring Caribbean storytellers, Christmas concerts and monthly music concerts are also held here. Also along the southern shore and reachable via one of the trails is a **military cemetery**, laid out at one of the island's few pieces of flat land. Shaded by tall trees, the weatherbeaten grey and white monuments date back to the late eighteenth century, and commemorate British soldiers and sailors who died defending St Lucia.

For more information on the park and Jazz Festival, contact the St Lucia National Trust (☎452-5005, Ⓦwww.slunatrust.org); see also p.198.

On the waterfront south of the fortifications, there's a small dock where you can catch the rather expensive tourist **ferries** (EC$25 one-way) to Rodney Bay Marina. Nearby, the *Jambe de Bois* restaurant (see p.188) is good for sandwiches and cold drinks, but with the variety and quality of restaurants close to Pigeon Island, perhaps not the best dinner choice. Two small but appealing **beaches**, equipped with toilets and shower facilities, lie to the east of the ferry dock. Both beaches are shallow and sheltered by rock jetties that provide calm water, and there are plenty of shady spots under the trees. All of Pigeon Island's beaches are particularly popular on weekends, when cruise ship passengers ferried in from Castries add to the usual crowd of locals enjoying a day out.

Several prominent hillocks dominate the island north of the military buildings; of these, 110-metre **Signal Hill** is the highest. A marked trail leads right to its base, and from there, it should take about fifteen minutes to reach the peak. It's easy to understand why Signal Hill was designated Pigeon Island's main lookout post: it affords panoramic vistas south to Gros Islet and the outskirts of Castries, and north over the expanse of the St Lucia Channel to the island of Martinique.

CAP ESTATE

Map 4, F2.

A couple of minutes' drive east of Pigeon Island, the coastal road winds a precipitous route to **CAP ESTATE**, a conspicuously upscale residential area distinguished by large villas and estates dotted into the hills east of the highway. The coastal views from anywhere along the road are expansive and compelling, and below lies the pretty **Becune Bay**. The beach is accessible by an obscure path found off the highway before you reach the second roundabout and the golf course (see below).

For details of accommodation in northern St Lucia,
see p.164; for eating and drinking, see p.187.

If you're after an ocean swim and some excellent snorkelling, head for **Smuggler's Cove**, a protected, cliff-lined, white sand beach accessed from the highway past the exclusive *LeSPORT* resort (see p.165); the steps that meander down a steep hill to the beach are on the right. Make sure to bring your own refreshments, as any beach bars here will be strictly monitored by the all-inclusive resorts of which they are a part. Back on the main road, to the south of the Cap Estate homes, is the ever-improving **St Lucia Golf and Country Club**, the island's only public course and a good one to boot – for more information, see p.215.

SALINE POINT AND THE NORTHERN TIP

Map 1, F1.

Several rough roads that strike off the highway around Cap Estate lead into the hills of St Lucia's northern tip, and to **Saline Point**, home to yet more large homes and vacation villas. Some of the peaks here reach as high as 150m and provide stunning coastal views – they're well worth the drive, and a regular car should get you everywhere you want to go in the dry season. The more remote **Pointe du Cap** – there are no signs but you'll know you're there when the road ends, replaced by the thundering ocean below – is a few minutes further along the coast. From here, St Lucia's nearest neighbour, Martinique, is just 40km away to the north.

Several dusty, unmarked dirt roads head east from Saline Point and Cap Estate toward **Pointe Hardy** on the north-east coast. Low-lying and scrubby enough to cope with the area's aridity, the liberal quantities of acacia thorn bushes, cacti and prickly pears are markedly different from the lush greenery of vegetation elsewhere on the island, and though you're unlikely to encounter one, the area is also home to a non-venomous boa constrictor. Dark with black and yellow patches, it is locally known as *tete chien*. Essentially, Pointe Hardy's desert-like quality means no tourists, no fences and no admission charges, and the area is ripe for exploration. The St Lucia National Trust is in the process of developing a conservation and eco-recreation site here (call ☎452-5005 or visit ⓦwww.slunatrust.org for an update), and there are several ad hoc **walking trails** lacing the area. Originally created by fishermen and farmers, the trails are not marked but are easy to follow, meandering around small hillocks and along the coast. To walk them, wear sturdy hiking shoes and bring lots of sun protections and water. If you don't want to go it alone, several companies offer **guided tours** of the area aboard 4WD vehicles (see p.220).

Soufrière and the
west coast

The west coast of St Lucia is incredibly beautiful, rich and varied in its attractions and notable for its pretty beaches, rural quality, and, in parts, decided lack of tourist traffic. You can search out isolated waterfalls, hike through astounding rainforest, swim, snorkel and scuba dive in secluded bays and visit peaceful fishing villages, all without the commercial feel of the northwest coast. However, the area does have its more blatant tourist draws, centred around Soufrière, where attractions, upmarket hotels and restaurants lend a bustling air of activity and touristic progress to the region.

Some 5km south of Castries and clustered around one of the Caribbean's most photographed coves, **Marigot Bay** is high on glamour but relatively low on visitors, and the settlement is little more than a handful of hotels and restaurants, most of them accessible solely by water taxi. South of Marigot is **Roseau valley**, noted for its wide river and extensive fields of bananas; as the home of the nation's largest **rum distillery**, it's also a worthwhile stop if you're interested in the production of the archetypal Caribbean spirit. Gathered around neat village greens and waterfronts lined with brightly coloured fishing boats, **Anse la Raye** and **Canaries** are convenient starting points for excursions to **waterfalls** in the nearby hills, accessed by easy or rigorous hikes. Anse La Raye also hosts a vibrant **street party** and fish fry on Friday nights.

The largest west coast settlement is the enduringly popular **Soufrière**, a small, unaffected and typically West Indian town that dwells in the shadows of the imposing **Pitons** and offers easy access to the island's celebrated central forest reserves (see Chapter 6). Just outside the town are the bubbling, odoriferous **La Soufrière Sulphur Springs**, vaunted as the world's only drive-in volcano and the most popular managed attraction that St Lucia has to offer. The land to the southeast of Soufrière was once taken up by massive sugar plantations, and many of the old estates have been opened up to tourists: **Morne Coubaril** gives an interesting insight into the slave era and offers hikes and guided horseback riding excursions through the countryside, while the **Diamond Botanical Gardens** boasts beautiful grounds, waterfalls and eighteenth-century mineral baths and the Font Doux estate offers a glimpse into life on a working cocoa plantation.

Getting there and around

A treacherously steep and twisting – though well-paved – road snakes along the southwest coast, making the trip from Castries to Soufrière an interesting drive. **Bus** service between the two towns is a labyrinthine affair. If you're based in Soufrière and want to travel to the capital, infrequent (particularly in the afternoon) buses along the west coast mean it's often easiest to first travel south to Vieux Fort and switch buses there for the final leg of the trip; you should allow the better part of a day for the journey. From

Soufrière to Vieux Fort, the bus fare is EC$7.50, and it's another EC$8.50 from Vieux Fort to Castries; direct services from Soufrière to Castries along the west coast cost EC$8.50. Buses also make runs along the west coast from Marigot, Anse la Raye and Canaries to Castries, and you'll pay less than EC$7 to get to the capital.

Taxis are easy to find, charging EC$160 from Castries to Soufrière, and EC$130 from Soufrière to Vieux Fort.

Marigot Bay to Canaries

A stretch of only 10km or so, the west coast between Marigot Bay and Canaries is peppered with quiet coastal villages that offer a refreshing alternative to more developed areas of the island. **Marigot Bay** is the only settlement with any kind of tourist infrastructure, and the few hotels and restaurants are perfectly placed to enjoy the natural beauty of this picture-perfect cove. The **Roseau Valley** offers some challenging riverbank hikes, and at the one-road fishing villages of **Anse la Raye** and **Canaries**, you can buy delicious snacks of grilled lobster, tiny *titiri* (fish fried whole) or head into the interior for a freshwater swim at one of several **waterfalls**.

MARIGOT BAY

Map 1, D6.

From the capital, the west-coast highway scoots through winding, hilly terrain and passes the signposted turnoff for nearby **Marigot Bay**; if you're travelling by bus, it's worth asking the driver if he'll make the three-minute detour down to the bay. There's no real town here, but there is a fistful of reclusive hotels and peaceful guesthouses strung along the bay's north and south sides. These, along with a couple of good restaurants and waterside bars from which to watch the sun set, and a few local shops, make up the village – Marigot isn't the island's busiest spot. The secluded feel is probably the main attraction for many, though, and it's a fine place to head for a relaxed swim and to take advantage of some dazzling panoramic photo opportunities. With massive, lushly vegetated hills enclosing the sea on three sides, Marigot's classic tropical appeal has long been recognized and has not escaped the notice of Hollywood – the bay was the setting for the 1967 film *Doctor Dolittle*, starring Rex Harrison. The sheltered inner lagoon, **Hurricane Hole**, is one of the best-protected natural yacht harbours on the island, and Marigot's waters are permanently dotted with boats of all shapes and sizes, some owned by the local Moorings charter company (see below) and others belonging to the "yachtie" crowd who congregate here.

For details of accommodation in Marigot Bay,
see p.166; for eating and drinking, see p.189.

From the coastal highway, Marigot's steep access road descends through the hills for about 2km ending abruptly at the compact waterfront. To the right is the ever-crowded jetty of **The Moorings Yacht Charters** (☏451-4357, ⓦwww.moorings.com) and clustered around the complex are the small **police station**, a **customs and immigration** office (☏452-3487) for incoming yachts, a **taxi stand** (☏453-4406) and the *Chateau Mygo* restaurant and shop. Set a few metres back from the waterfront are entrances to the brace of small hotels set high in the hills overlooking the bay, and accessed via a walkway to your left is *The Shack* (see p.189) – one of the best, and most reasonable, restaurants around.

Though a sign above the marina jetty reads "Welcome to the *Marigot Beach Club*", the club and its **beach** (the bay's best swimming spot) are actually a few hundred yards across the bay, accessible 24 hours a day via a small ferry boat (EC$3 round trip); the five-minute trip takes you directly to the palm-lined seashore. Slung along a short and thin promontory that juts into the bay from the hotel restaurant, the beach is nonetheless spacious, with calm surf, plenty of shade and good snorkelling to its west side. Refreshments are available from *Doolittle's* restaurant and bar (see p.189) – an excellent place to watch the sunset – and the hotel also operates a watersports concession. Visitors in general – and women travelling alone in particular - should be aware that there are several persistent marijuana hawkers who hang around both sides of the bay; although they may seem a little threatening at first, a persistent "no thanks" should send them off.

ROSEAU VALLEY

Map 1, D6.

South of Marigot Bay, the highway winds and dips through the sharp west coast hills to the next settled area, **Roseau**, a fertile lowlands valley extensively planted with fields of bananas, dotted with small settlements and home to St Lucia's largest **rum distillery**, which you can tour with Sunlink (see p.220).

To the east of the factory is a series of **waterfalls** along the Roseau River, but as agricultural chemicals from the banana plantations have been found in the water, swimming is inadvisable. The trip to the cascades makes a pleasant walk in itself, but you'll have to go with a guide – there are no trails as such, and the terrain can get pretty rough. Following the banks of the river is not a good idea as there are several spots where you have to detour away from the water, and you'll want to avoid traipsing through private property. To find a reliable **guide**, you can call the forestry department in Castries (☎450-2231) on the off-chance that a ranger will want to take you, or ask around once you're at the valley; several local people will take visitors to the falls for around US$25 per person. Also of note here is the Community of Roseau's **church**, which features some fine *omeros* murals of the black madonna by local artist Dunstan St Omer.

The rum distillery

Sunlink's very touristy "Rhythm of Rum Tour" takes you to the island's largest **rum distillery** (you have to visit as part of a pre-arranged tour), where the past is recreated through the re-enactment of street scenes and daily life in plantation times. Gimmickry aside, the factory tour is interesting (and smelly) enough, explaining the importance of rum in the island's past while demonstrating the production processes of today. Visitors are given the chance to both sample and buy some freshly distilled island rum. Sunlink (☎452 8232, ⊕www.sunlinktours.com) offer this tour from Castries, in conjunction with their trip to Marigot Bay for US$40 per person.

ANSE LA RAYE AND CANARIES

Map 1, C6–B8.

Heading further south, the roads passes two typical coastal communities – **Anse la Raye** and **Canaries** – both centred around small beaches bobbing with wooden fishing boats. Though there's not much of interest in either settlement, to the east of both are rivers studded with waterfalls, which offer a refreshing alternative to saltwater swimming.

About 2km south of Roseau, **ANSE LA RAYE** is bisected by the west coast highway, which becomes the village's main drag once you enter town. Crowded with vendors sitting behind haphazard piles of fruit, the narrow streets that spread back from here are lined with somewhat weatherbeaten homes, and though the town is pretty and the people generally welcoming, there aren't any really compelling sights. A tidy village green fronts a small **beach**, chock-full of brightly painted fishing boats and drying nets; you might also see fishermen hauling in the flat, long-tailed skates after which the village is named.

Spurred on by the popularity of the jump-up in Gros Islet, Anse la Raye hosts a **fish fry** every Friday night. It's a much smaller affair than its northern counterpart, with more emphasis on eating and drinking at big communal tables in the main street than going crazy until the wee hours – here, proceedings are at their liveliest from around 9pm till midnight. The variety of seafood – from lobster and *titiri* to *lambi* and dolphin – is more expansive and expensive than in Gros Islet, but at EC$10 for a chargrilled tuna steak, some corn, a hot bake and a large rum and coke, it's still cheaper – and more fun – than anything else around.

Spanned by a small metal bridge, the **Anse la Raye River** empties into the ocean just south of town, and a fifteen-minute walk along its banks from the bridge brings you to the fifteen-metre **River Rock waterfall** (EC$5) with natural swimming pools at the base, picnic tables, a changing area and a bar serving beer and soft drinks. Despite the amenities, it's way off the beaten tourist track and you'll often find you only have to share the place with a few locals if you don't have it all to yourself.

A further 4km south along the highway is the signposted turnoff for the small fishing village of **CANARIES**, thought to have been named after the Arawak *kanawes*, or clay cooking pots, which have been found in the area. Once you've cast your eye over the boat-dotted beach, head south to the six or so **waterfalls** along the **Canaries River**. Though – as with the falls on the Roseau River – forestry department rangers might be persuaded to act as guides (see p.139), the simplest way to find someone to take you there is to ask around the village; you'll pay at least US$25 per person. South of the river is the St Lucia National Trust camping site at **Anse la Liberté** (see p.153), to which you can drive or take a boat from the Canaries waterfront (about EC$5).

Soufrière and around

Officially established in 1746, **SOUFRIÈRE** is the oldest town in St Lucia, and was the island's capital under French rule. Naturally framed by hills and dominated by the looming, conical Pitons – twin volcanic peaks thrusting straight out of the sea to the south of the town – Soufrière's deep **bay** is extremely picturesque, particularly when viewed from the hilly coastal roads as you enter town from the north or south. This unspoiled allure has often drawn the attention of film producers: scenes from *Superman II*, *Water* and *White Squall* were shot in and around town.

Nestled on the island's southwest coast halfway between Castries and Vieux Fort, Soufrière is perfectly placed for **day trips** to popular **natural attractions** and **plantation tours**, which are all within minutes of downtown and easily accessed via public transport. The Soufrière surrounds also boast some marvellous **beaches**, many of which have black sand left over from past volcanic activity, and the local waters contain some of St Lucia's prettiest **reefs**; in 1994, a marine park was created here to help preserve the delicate ecosystems and to alleviate the pressure put on marine resources by hotels, diving operators and fishermen attempting to feed a growing population. Though Soufrière is generally an unpretentious kind of place, it is heavily visited and not unaffected by tourism. You'll probably be approached by craft vendors and would-be guides, and some local people will ask for a couple of dollars for giving directions, but the attention is not overpowering and is easily dealt with by a polite "no thanks" if you're not interested.

Arrival and getting around

Taxis and **buses** heading to and from Castries, Vieux Fort and the east coast cluster around Soufrière's town square and the waterfront (for details see p.28). The latter is also the place to hop aboard the convenient **water taxis** that traverse the area: boats service all of the nearby bays, many of which are difficult to access from the land without your own car. Water taxis also offer **sightseeing trips** to Castries and back – at US$350 for four, the trips are expensive but exotic. One-way trips (no sightseeing) for four or more people start at US$90–100.

For tours, snorkelling trips and boats to Castries,
contact a member of the water taxi association
(☏454-5420) at the waterfront.

THE TOWN

Map 5.

The largest settlement of the southwest coast, **Soufrière** is a quiet place today, charming in its lack of polish and filled with a melange of architectural styles ranging from slapped-together wooden fishing huts to modern cement blocks. Some buildings, particularly those around the town square, recall the ornate facades of French colonial days.

Soufrière's **tourist office** (Mon–Fri 8am–4pm, Sat 8am–noon; ⊤459-7419), on the waterfront and across from the main pier, is a handy source of local information – staff can also direct you to members of the tourism department's helpful **guide corps**, who are uniformed in blue T-shirts and give walking tours of the town. Soufrière is small enough to explore on foot, and the abundance of jammed one-way streets and the lack of parking render vehicles inadvisable in any case. An obvious starting point is the pretty **waterfront**, a jumble of piers and boat slips where local fishing craft and tourist party-boats dock, and where you'll find a small **fish market**, housed in a blue building behind the *Old Courthouse Restaurant*. The **fruit and vegetable market** is a more haphazard affair, with piles of produce sold right on the waterfront and the surrounding streets. A well-maintained walkway runs along the northern waterfront, where ornate streetlamps, benches and poinciana trees make for a pleasant evening stroll. The promenade ends near a small **crafts centre** (Mon–Sat 9am–4pm), where local artisans sell carvings, straw hats and the like at a reasonable price. Next door is the office of the **Soufrière Regional Development Foundation** (⊤459-7200), a regional planning agency working toward sustainable development of the tourism industry; displays inside focus on the local fishing industry and the **Soufrière Marine Management Authority** (⊤459-5500, ⊛www.smma.org), guardians of the Soufrière marine park.

At the north end of the waterfront, on Bridge Street, the town **cemetery** has been in continuous use since 1743 – the raised cement crypts are faded and occasionally crumbling. North of here, a long, dark-sand **beach** is overlooked by a couple of hotels. The beach is pleasant, though not very wide, and you can use the shower and pool of the *Hummingbird* hotel for a small fee – however, there are better places to swim just out of town (see p.207).

A block east of the waterfront, hemmed in by Bridge Street to the west and Church Street to the east, is the big and grassy **town square**, laid out by Soufrière's original French inhabitants in the eighteenth century, and, notoriously, the scene of numerous **executions** by guillotine during the dark days of the Revolution. It's a peaceful and shady space today, though, bordered by businesses and homes built in the classic French colonial style with second-floor balconies and intricate decorative woodwork. The J.Q. Charles dry goods store at the square's southwest corner is one of the more ornate, with fretwork patterned after snowflakes. Dominating the east end of the square is the **Lady of Assumption Church**, built in 1953 on the site of several older churches destroyed by earthquakes and fire. Soufrière has what might be viewed as bad-weather karma: the town was pummelled by hurricanes in 1780, 1817, 1831, 1898 and 1980, and by an earthquake in 1839, while in 1955, half the town was razed to the ground by a fire.

For details of accommodation in and around Soufrière, see pp.167–171; for eating and drinking, see p.190.

Nearby beaches

Map 1, B9–B10.

To the immediate north of Soufrière is the popular **Anse Chastanet beach** – long, wide and presided over by the resort of the same name (see p.167). With a pristine reef within swimming distance, Anse Chastanet offers some of

St Lucia's best **snorkelling**. It's also a great starting point for scuba excursions, with several good **dive sites** nearby; the dive shop *Scuba St Lucia* (Ⓦwww.scubastlucia.com), right on the beach, rents scuba equipment as well as snorkelling gear. Anse Chastanet is reachable via a deplorably bad, pothole-filled road, jutting right from the main road just before you enter Soufrière from the north. The 2km tracks takes about 15 minutes by car or 45 minutes on foot, or you can catch a water taxi from Soufrière (US$10 one way). Also reachable by water taxi from town are two pretty, secluded beaches to the north of Anse Chastanet, **Anse Mamin** – where visitors can try jungle biking (Ⓦwww.bikestlucia.com) through miles of hilly terrain – and **Anse Jambon**.

SOUFRIÈRE ESTATE AND DIAMOND BOTANICAL GARDENS

Map 5, F5, G4.

With rich, productive soil fertilized in part by past volcanic activity, the Soufrière environs represent some of St Lucia's most heavily cultivated land. The French were the first to set up **plantations** in the area to grow sugar cane, bananas and limes, but today, farming has mostly been reduced to small-scale plots. However, remnants of the plantations still exist: about 2km east of Soufrière town, along the inland road to the hamlet of Fond St Jacques, **Soufrière Estate** is a former eighteenth-century sugar plantation that was originally part of a 2000-acre land grant bestowed by Louis XIV to the Devaux family in 1713. The family was responsible for much of the development in the area, and are today still prominent hoteliers and landowners.

Most of the land is private nowadays, but part of the former sugar plantation can be explored in the **Diamond**

Botanical Gardens (Mon–Sat 10am–5pm, Sun 10am–3pm; EC$7; ☏459-7565 or 459-7155), well worth a visit, with mineral baths and a waterfall contained in lush grounds. The large, manicured **gardens** are networked by well-marked and easy-to-follow paths and packed with dozens of labelled tropical species, including brilliant hibiscus in red, pink and white, yellow allamanda, sweet-smelling frangipani trees, the oddly shaped lobster claw and a number of different palms, as well as cocoa trees, tall Norfolk pines and elaborate casuarinas and flamboyants. There's also a Japanese water garden, on a side path that loops back to the main walkway, with small and ethereal arrangements of flowers and trees laid out in classic Japanese style. Brochures containing maps are available at the admission desk for an extra charge of EC$2.50.

The main path through the gardens follows the thin Diamond River to a sibilant ten-metre **cascade** fed by a mix of natural streams and underground thermal sulphur springs from the La Soufrière volcano. Splashing over rocks and shimmering with different colours caused by the sulphur content, the waterfall is aesthetic but unfortunately unsuitable for swimming due to agricultural pollution in the water.

Adjacent to the waterfall, the thermal **mineral baths** are built on the site of the original facilities commissioned by Louis XIV in 1784. Then-governor Baron de Laborie discovered the estate's hot springs and sent water samples to Paris to be analyzed; they were found to contain the same levels of allegedly curative minerals as in Aix-les-Bains in France and Aachen in Germany, and Louis XIV ordered baths to be built for his troops. Rebuilt by Andre deBoulay in 1925, they are said to cure ailments such as rheumatism and arthritis; some people still drink the waters, believing this to be a more direct route to curing internal ills. The first spa buildings were destroyed after the Revolution, but it's possible to see their crumbling remnants in an overgrown hole behind the bath house. Today, you can splash about in the slightly pungent depths of an outdoor pool or in several smaller tubs inside the bathhouse; the water is cooled from its high in-ground temperatures, but it's still comfortably warm. In addition to the main entry fee to the complex, you'll pay EC$6.50 to use the pool and EC$10 for a private bath. Adjacent to the baths is a small **bar** selling drinks, snacks and sweets alongside souvenirs.

Toraille Falls

Map 1, C10. Daily 9am–5pm. EC$5.

Further down the road towards Fond St Jacques and the rainforest, about ten minutes from Soufrière, lies a gorgeous 15-metre **waterfall** set in a tropical garden. You can bring a bottle of bubbly and sit in the pool beneath the cascade or on benches, or hike the upper trail behind the fall, where hummingbirds, ginger lilies and a stunning view of Petit Piton vie for attention. Come early in the morning or late in the afternoon to avoid the coach-tour crowds.

MORNE COUBARIL ESTATE

Map 5, D7. Daily 9am–4.30pm. ⓉΤ459-7340, Ⓦwww.coubaril.com.

Less than a kilometre south of Soufrière on the road to Vieux Fort, **Morne Coubaril** is a 250-acre working plantation that has been opened up as a rather questionable tourist attraction. Promising to reveal a "way of life in the good old days", the thirty-minute walking **tours** are conducted by guides clad in eighteenth-century plantation garb – meaning the clothing worn by house slaves. Nonetheless, viewing the fields of cocoa, copra and cassava provides an interesting insight into tropical cultivation, and there's plenty of explanation from the guides.

Also on site are recreations of thatch-roofed Amerindian huts, as well as a small working sugar mill and several snack and gift shops, but perhaps the best aspect of Coubaril is the guided **hikes**, which include a two-hour trek that starts at the Diamond Botanical Gardens (see p.107), taking in the forest, waterfalls and thermal pools, and ending at the Morne Coubaril hill in the estate grounds. Full-day and half-day **horseback tours** of the plantation and the surrounding area are also available. Tours and rides are available through select operators only – call the St Lucia Tourist Board (☎452-4094) or Sunlink Tours (☎452-0511) for more information.

LA SOUFRIÈRE SULPHUR SPRINGS

Map 5, E6. Daily 9am–5pm. EC$3.

Misleadingly billed as the world's only drive-in volcano, **La Soufrière Sulphur Springs**, a short drive south of Soufrière town off the road to Vieux Fort, was a **volcano** some 13km in diameter before it erupted and collapsed into itself around 40,000 years ago. La Soufrière remains active to this day – theoretically, it could erupt any time – but as it is now classified as a **solfatara**, meaning it emits gases and vapours rather than lava and hot ash, a molten shower is extremely unlikely. La Soufrière has long been a place of myth and superstition: despite the fact that there's little evidence of such activity in their culture, old and dubious legends claim that Arawak Indians used the site for human sacrifice, while the querulous but evidently cautious Caribs are thought to have called it *Qualibou*, meaning "a place of death".

Turn into the springs at the signed road and you'll know you're in the midst of a volcano – killed off by sulphuric emissions, the vegetation becomes sparse and an eggy odour

Reduit Beach

Produce market, Castries

Fregate Islands Nature Reserve

View of the Pitons from the Anse Chastenet Resort

Plantation, Cul de Sac Valley

Carnival revellers

GREG EVANS

Fishing boats, Soufrière

IAN CUMMING/AXIOM

Barre de L'Isle Trail

hangs in the air. After leaving your vehicle in the car park just metres from the most active part of the volcanic area, official – and very informative – guides will walk you up to the **viewing platforms** that overlook sections of the crater, seven barren acres of steaming, bubbling pools of sulphur-dense water and rocks tinged green and yellow. The pervasive acrid smell is perhaps La Soufrière's most memorable aspect, something like rotting onions in an omelette gone bad. Some years ago, visitors were allowed to walk across the crater, but this practice was stopped when one of the guides fell through a fissure – though sustaining severe burns, he lived to tell the tale. Now, goats occasionally hop across the pools and rocks, cheerfully oblivious of how close they are to becoming stew.

FOND DOUX ESTATE

Map 5, G6. Daily 9am-5pm. EC$10. ☏459-7545.

Set back from the main Soufrière–Vieux Fort road, 3km from La Soufriere and just south of Ladera, **Fond Doux** is a gorgeous 250-year old **working cocoa estate** whose produce is sold to local grocers in the form of cocoa sticks, and to Hershey's as the base for their famous chocolate. In the late eighteenth century, the estate was also home to a huge battle between recently liberated St Lucian brigands and the Imperialist British; the latter suffered heavy losses and were forced to flee. Musket balls have been found on site, and knowledgeable guides will show you these, as well as the extensive gardens and the plantation itself, on an informal but informative walking tour. The discussion of the cocoa-making process is a definite highlight, and visitors get to sample the raw, bitter pods straight from the tress, as well as visit the cocoa ovens used to dry them, and the "cocoa dancing" shed, where men dance on the beans with their bare feet to polish them, making them shiny

FOND DOUX ESTATE

enough to be bagged and exported to Hershey's and elsewhere. There is an excellent local **restaurant** (9am–4pm) on site and a local juice or punch is included in the entrance fee.

THE PITONS

Map 1, B10, B11.

Heading back on the main road from Fond Doux to Soufrière, the majestic peaks of the **Pitons** tower above sea level, dominating the southwest coast. Visible on a clear day from as far north as the hills of Castries, these two breathtaking cones are undoubtedly St Lucia's most photographed feature. Overlooking the south side of Soufrière's harbour, the northern peak is Petit Piton; south of Petit is Gros Piton, wider at the base but similar in height. Maps give varying elevations for each of the peaks, some even claiming that Petit is taller than Gros Piton, but the St Lucian government figures of 734m (2460ft) and 798m (2620ft) respectively are generally accepted.

Beyond their aesthetic appeal, the Pitons offer an opportunity – literally – for high adventure. **Petit Piton** has been scaled in the past, and though the climb is discouraged by local authorities – there are fragile ecosystems to take into account, as well as the inherent difficulty and danger of climbing a near-vertical slab of rock – some seem willing to clamber up nonetheless. However, this is both irresponsible and inadvisable – if you must go, hiring a guide from the town is essential; ask at the tourist office or at the Regional Development Foundation (℡459-5500).

Gros Piton, while still a challenge, is more manageable for **hiking**. It's a long and hot ascent nonetheless (bring sunscreen, plenty of water and something to eat), and you'll need to start out in the cool of early morning to ensure that you're able to get back down before nightfall. As the path branches off in several places, a guide is necessary; the Soufrière Regional Development Foundation in town (see opposite) will usually be able to find someone for you, and you'll pay about US$50 per person. Depending on your level of fitness, the hike will take three to six hours each way. It starts out low and level along a rudimentary, rocky path and gently ascends until about 300m from the peak, from whereon it's a steep, rocky climb – there are tree trunks and brush to hang on to. The peak itself is a wide, level area with marvellous views: on a clear day you'll see the neighbouring islands of St Vincent to the south and Martinique to the north, as well as planes taking off from the island's airports in both Vieux Fort and Castries.

If climbing a mountain under the sun's glare doesn't appeal, head for **Anse des Pitons beach**, which separates the twin peaks and provides stunning views of both. Home to the *Jalousie Hilton* resort (non-guests are admitted; see p.168), the beach is several shades lighter than most in the area as the gleaming white sand was imported specially from Guyana at a cost of US$1 million to impress the mostly upscale clientele. The sand looks rather anomalous, and unless the *Hilton* is able to mitigate the forces of nature, it's sure to be swiftly depleted by wave action.

On the south side of the *Jalousie Hilton* property is the **Pitons Warm Mineral Waterfall** (daily 6.30am–7pm; US$1), a pleasantly tepid mix of spring water and thermal volcanic emissions cascading down 30m into a natural pool, which makes for an energizing swim. If you're driving, turn in at the sign for the hotel, from where the route to the falls is marked – you can also take a water taxi to the beach from Soufrière town (around US$15).

THE PITONS

The south coast

St Lucia's southern coast boasts some striking scenery: south of Soufrière, the thin mountain road whirls and dips inland before swinging toward the ocean to reveal a string of coastal villages and, ultimately, the island's second largest town, Vieux Fort, all framed by the towering ranges of the central forest reserve. This southwest corner was once an Amerindian stronghold, and petroglyphs have been found throughout the area, suggesting a long and fruitful habitation by the Arawaks and Caribs. After Europeans arrived, the area became home to large plantations producing bananas, coconuts, cocoa and sugar cane, and some southern villages and towns were minor commerce and shipping centres. These days, the large plantations have been replaced by smaller farms and fishing enterprises.

Despite the fact that nearly all foreign visitors arrive in the south, at Vieux Fort's Hewanorra International Airport, there's little in the way of tourist activity in this part of the island and large resorts are almost non-existent. Appealing places to swim are few and far between, and those bays that do line the coast are mostly of the dark volcanic sand that doesn't match up to the conventional stereotype of a Caribbean seashore. In many ways, though, this is the attraction – it's a quieter, more residential part of the island, a world away from the tourism strongholds of the north and west. Indeed, with its beaches, natural attractions and an adequate number of places to stay (all easily accessible from Hewanorra Airport), it's surprising the area hasn't become more popular.

Several kilometres southwest of Soufriere, **Choiseul** is a small and somewhat faded fishing village, wrapped around a picture-postcard shore, and is best known for its Arts and Craft Development Centre, a cooperative selling locally made carvings, baskets and pottery. South of Choiseul, un-hyped tours of the lush 150-acre **Balenbouche Estate** have none of the demeaning costumes and prepared speeches of the more contrived, tourist-oriented plantations in busier parts of St Lucia.

Further along the southwest coast, near the island's southern tip, the plains and gently sloping hills around **Vieux Fort** stand in stark contrast to the mountainous terrain of the north. While the town itself is crowded and not particularly attractive, the coast east of the city hosts one of the island's finest beaches at **Anse de Sables**, a long, wide stretch of golden sand popular with windsurfers and sunbathers. The beach falls within the boundaries of the proposed **Pointe Sable National Park**, a gorgeous collection of mangroves, beaches, rocky promontories, protected nature grounds and, offshore, the fascinating **Maria Islands Nature Reserve**.

Arrival, transport and information

Most visitors arrive in St Lucia at **Hewanorra International Airport** in Vieux Fort, and onward transportation throughout the island is readily available – if somewhat slow – from here. Your first stop should be the **tourist office** (Mon–Fri 7am–last flight, Sat & Sun 10am–last flight; ☏454-6644) just outside the arrival area, where you can pick up brochures and maps and get the lowdown on the latest official taxi rates. There are half a dozen **car rental** booths at the airport, open daily from 8am until the last flight, which can arrive as late as 10pm. Also on the concourse, and directly outside the arrival area, is a **taxi** stand. Taxis to Castries from the airport or anywhere in Vieux Fort travel the wide and slick east coast highway and turn inland toward the capital at Dennery. The **fare** to Castries is EC$140, and the 58km trip takes a bit more than an hour. Vieux Fort to Soufrière is EC$150, and the 42km ride takes forty minutes to an hour, depending upon your driver's tolerance level for steep, winding roads. Vieux Fort to Gros Islet costs EC$180.

Travelling around the south by **bus** is time-consuming and not particularly easy. Like taxis, buses run from Vieux Fort to Castries along the east coast highway, and to Soufrière along the west coast road. Services, between 6.30am and 10.30pm during the week, are much reduced on weekends. **East coast buses** to Castries leave from New Dock Road on the south side of the airport: turn right out of the airport, follow the road past Anse de Sables beach to a traffic roundabout, where you'll see a large soccer field, the Cable & Wireless building and the bus stand across the road. For **west coast buses** to Soufrière, turn right out of the airport, right again at the junction, and the bus stand is on the left at Clarke Street, next to a Shell service station and traffic light. You'll pay EC$8.50 to travel to northern St Lucia.

For details of accommodation in the south, see pp.171–173;
for eating and drinking, see p.193.

CHOISEUL AND AROUND

Map 1, C12.

South of Soufrière, the west coast road meanders through

hilly inland terrain, passing several small settlements before descending abruptly toward the coast and the French administrative Quarter of Choiseul, named for the compact village of **CHOISEUL** itself: the turnoff is on the right, just past a white Anglican church. This is a quiet place, with little to see or do save swimming by the beach or river and exploring the pretty waterfront, with its Catholic church and fish market directly on the beach.

Choiseul is bordered to the south by the **River Dorée**, and to the north by a small oceanside settlement called **Caribe Point**, which was home to the last of St Lucia's Caribs until the nineteenth century, by which time intermarriage had made pure Carib ancestry a rarity. A few of their descendents still live here, some in thatched huts reminiscent of traditional Amerindian dwellings. Two minutes' drive north of the Choiseul waterfront is the dark-sand **Choiseul Community Beach**, a wide seashore with plenty of shade under the trees and lots of space for the volleyball court that's a favourite haunt amongst the village's youth.

Moving south from Choiseul, the highway runs parallel to the coastal plain for a kilometre or so before entering the small satellite settlement of **LA FARGUE**, best known for the **Choiseul Arts and Craft Development Centre** (Mon–Sat; call ☎459-3226 for opening hours), on the right of the road just past *Miss Lucy's Mini Guesthouse*. This is probably the best place on the south coast to buy locally produced crafts – prices are better than those at the tourist shops of larger towns and the range here is huge. Artisans display their pottery, mats, carvings, wicker baskets and traditional wood furniture in the main building.

Further along the Soufrière–Vieux Fort Road lies the **Saltibus waterfall and trail**, reached via the last turn-off on the main road before the well signposted Balenbouche Estate (see p.118). A worthwhile stop, the trail is a strenuous but rewarding hour-and-a-quarter hike through rainforest to the waterfall, where there are a variety of pleasant pools in which to bathe.

BALENBOUCHE ESTATE

Map 1, C13. Daily 9am–5pm. EC$5. ⓉP455-1244, Ⓦwww.balenbouche.com.

Around 3km south of Choiseul village, the coastal highway crosses the River Dorée and passes the signed driveway leading into **Balenbouche Estate**, a 150-acre property spread around a charming nineteenth-century **plantation house**, white with a peaked roof and a wraparound porch. Though it's small in comparison to the great houses of other St Lucian estates, the house is large enough to serve as both owner Uta Lawaetz's home and as a **guesthouse** (see p.172). About one third of the grounds are farmed (crops are sold at local markets), and much of the property is permanently shaded by massive calabash, flamboyant, mango, breadfruit and banyan trees. Also on site are a defunct watermill dating from 1780 and the remains of an old sugar mill, embedded in the ground and surrounded by serpentine tree trunks.

The estate stretches right down to the ocean, and a short walk toward the coast takes you to the **Balenbouche River**, which cuts through the property and is a lovely spot for a little away-from-it-all meditation. Along the shore are several soccer ball-sized rocks with smoothed basins hollowed into their tops, which are believed to have been used by Arawaks as washing stones. The various **petroglyph** sites inland along the river further attest to a strong Amerindian presence in the area. If you want to see them, ask at the great house for a guide; you'll pay about EC$10 per person. From the Balenbouche great house, you can also walk to **Anse Touloulou beach** in about fifteen minutes, following the river banks and ascending a low hillock. The beach is small and secluded with good swimming and gentle surf.

The best way to explore Balenbouche is to join one of the relaxed, informal **walking tours** of the plantation (EC$10). Normally conducted by the owner or her equally-knowledgable daughter, these informative tours are usually available on request. Good, healthy, homemade food is also on offer – if you think you would like to stay in Balenbouche for lunch, call ahead.

LABORIE

Map 1, D13.

The last village along the road before Vieux Fort, tiny **LABORIE** is skirted by the west coast road and has a pleasant bay packed with fishing boats and an oceanside **market**. On the inland side of the road just north of the village turnoff, a sign points up a steep and rocky hill to the **Le Blanc Nature Heritage** site. Driving up the potholed road to the top of Morne Le Blanc is an act of faith, but the reward for the ten-minute journey is wide **views** of Vieux Fort and the southeast and west coasts. There are two viewing platforms here – be careful when climbing the platforms, though, as they appear not to have been attended to for some years.

VIEUX FORT

Map 1, E13.

Jammed with traffic and produce vendors, **VIEUX FORT** is St Lucia's second largest town and its most southerly settlement, a busy commercial centre and the base for businesses that service sprawling **Hewanorra International Airport**, just north of downtown. Both the town and the airport lie on a relatively flat plain that slopes gently toward the north and the south-central mountains, and as the southern tip of St Lucia comes to a point around Vieux Fort, the runway stretches – literally – from the east to the west coast of the island.

Until the early seventeenth century, the area around Vieux Fort was inhabited by the **Arawaks**, who are thought to have grown crops in the fertile plains that spread out beneath the interior mountains. Vieux Fort later came into prominence as a replenishing point for Dutch shippers, who built a small fort east of town on a promontory now called **Pointe Sable** to protect their supplies from the Caribs, thus giving the town its name – "Old Fort" in French. Encroaching European expansion saw the arrival of large-scale cultivation – relatively flat land, an abundance of fresh water and soil rich from volcanic activity made the area suitable for growing **sugar cane**, and by the mid-eighteenth century, there were more than sixty estates in the area. The great plantations lasted throughout the slavery years until the 1920s, when sugar cane prices plummeted in the face of the cheaper and more easily produced beet sugar from other countries. Prosperity came to the area again during World War II, when Allied forces leased one thousand acres of land around Vieux Fort (which encompassed the St Jude Hospital, still in use today), and built a military base and the airstrip which was later enlarged to become Hewanorra. There's still evidence of military construction in the unusually wide roads surrounding the airport, presumably laid to accommodate large military convoys and equipment.

- -

Reviews of accommodation in the Vieux Fort area
start on p.172; for eating and drinking, see p.193.

- -

Downtown Vieux Fort lies a couple of minutes' drive south of the airport. The best place to savour the urban

VIEUX FORT

bustle is the main drag, **Clarke Street**, lined with shops and homes embellished with gingerbread fretwork in the classic colonial style. A small, grassy square along Clarke Street has a **bandstand**, which serves as an occasional venue for St Lucia Jazz Festival performances, while the west side of downtown is bordered by a small, businesslike waterfront where fishing boats pull up on shore, but overall, there's little to do or see.

Each May, St Lucia Jazz Festival concerts are held in and around Vieux Fort – for more details, see p.198.

POINTE SABLE NATIONAL PARK

Map 1, F12–F14, G12.

Just outside Vieux Fort, the proposed land mass for **POINTE SABLE NATIONAL PARK** stretches along the southeastern coastline for some 7km, encompassing the **Cape Moule à Chique** promontory, **Anse de Sables beach**, the **Man Kòtè Mangrove** and the **Savannes Bay Nature Reserve**, as well as the offshore **Maria Islands**. Sponsored by the St Lucia National Trust, the park is awaiting official status and remains undeveloped – the areas are not yet fully regulated nor particularly well cared for – but the Trust's efforts to preserve the seagrass beds, mangrove swamps and coral reefs are slowly coming to fruition.

Cape Moule à Chique

Map 1, F14.

At the southern outskirts of downtown Vieux Fort, the large and hilly promontory of **Cape Moule à Chique** (233m) juts into the sea, forming St Lucia's most southerly point and framing the industrial port on Vieux Fort Bay, an

POINTE SABLE NATIONAL PARK

inlet with storage warehouses and massive docks for large cargo ships. To get to Cape Moule à Chique, drive to the roundabout and bear left onto New Dock Road, then turn left again at the Cable & Wireless station on the hill. There is a place to park at the point's working **lighthouse**, where you'll have views of the east coast, the expansive Anse de Sables beach and the two offshore Maria Islands (see opposite), as well as the interior mountains.

Anse de Sables

Map 1, F14.

Stretching some 2km north from the cliffs of Cape Moule à Chique to Pointe Sable, the **Anse de Sables beach** is the only real option for swimming near Vieux Fort. A favoured spot for windsurfers thanks to mild surf, good breezes and the presence of a branch of the European windsurfing school, Club Mistral (daily Nov–June 8.30am–5pm; Ⓦwww.club-mistral.com) at its southern end. The expansive seashore itself is a clean and golden treat, free from the overcrowding and noise of some of the beaches in the north of the island. There is virtually no trees for shade, however, and no toilet or changing facilities except those at several cheerful oceanside bars and restaurants serving cheap burgers, fish and beer.

At the south end of the beach, in the shadow of the looming Cape Moule à Chique, is the **Maria Islands Interpretive Centre** (Mon–Fri 9am–4.30pm; ☎454-5014), a small natural history centre, which is the focal point for the National Trust's efforts on the south coast as well as the place to arrange a trip to the nearby Maria Islands (see p.123). The one-room **museum** (free) provides an interesting insight into local ecosystems and history, with displays on Amerindian culture (including skeletal remains and a skull found in the area), as well as on mangroves and marine life; the fishing industry section has an example of a traditional dugout canoe called a *gonmyé*.

South of Pointe Sable, at Beanfield, the seashore is known as **Cloudnest Beach**, and there are a couple of hotels and beach bars as well as a small **fish market**. The beach at this end is okay, but as fishermen tend to be busy here, you're better off doing your sunbathing a few hundred metres south at the section called **Sandy Beach**. Though this is the most popular spot on the bay (particularly on weekends, when townspeople descend), the paucity of tourists along the south coast means that the sand is rarely crowded, and you're likely to share it only with the occasional vendor wandering along selling straw hats or aloe for sunburn. Cold drinks and restrooms are available at the *Sandy Beach Club* next door, and the nearby *Reef* beach bar rents beach chairs (EC$5 for the day) as well as serving decent food.

Maria Islands Nature Reserve

Map 1, F14. Sept–April

A kilometre or so off the Anse de Sables shore are the two scrubby, windswept cays that comprise the **Maria Islands Nature Reserve**. Both the hilly, 24-acre **Maria Major** and its smaller sister islet, 4-acre **Maria Minor**, are breeding areas for numerous **sea birds**, including the booby and frigate, and are home to two species of reptiles, one of which – the **kouwés snake** (also spelled "couresse") – is found nowhere else in the world. About a metre long with dark green and brown markings, this harmless snake once thrived on the mainland, but was eradicated by the mongooses introduced by sugar-cane planters to kill off cane rats, mice and snakes. Today, *kouwés* live only on Maria

Major and number a mere one hundred or so. At around 35cm long with a bright blue tail and a yellow belly, the male *zandoli tè*, or **ground lizard**, is also found only on the Maria Islands and nearby Praslin Island on the east coast, where some of their number were transferred due to the extreme aridity of the Marias in the dry season. The less ostentatious female is brown with darker vertical stripes.

There's a short but comely **beach** of golden sand on Maria Major, with a **reef** a few metres offshore, making this a good spot for swimming and snorkelling. Several unmarked and unchallenging **trails** loop around the islands, taking you past sparse, cactus-strewn vegetation and rocky shoreline. It's difficult to get lost on such tiny pieces of land, but in any event, no one is allowed on the Marias without an **authorized guide** from the St Lucia National Trust (see below). They lead you through the trails in search of *kouwés* and *zandoli tè* and will identify the flora and fauna on hand.

Visiting the islands

If you want to **visit** the Marias, you'll need to phone or call in at the **Maria Islands Interpretive Centre** (Mon–Fri 9am–4.30pm; ☎454-5014) at the south end of Anse de Sables beach (see p.122). This is the only place where you can arrange a day trip conducted by official National Trust guides. Costing EC$94 for one person, EC$80.40 per person for groups of two or more, the trips begin at the centre and consist of **walking tours** of the islands as well as stops for swimming and snorkelling (bring your own gear). Though you can arrange Saturday or Sunday trips, the centre is open only on weekdays, and its hours can be erratic – it's always best to call ahead. Lastly, note that the islands are closed to visitors between May and July/August every year, when several species of birds are nesting.

Man Kòtè Mangrove and Savannes Bay Nature Reserve

Map 1, F12–13, G12.

Some 3km from Vieux Fort and just north of Pointe Sable, the coastal highway toward Dennery passes a signposted turnoff marked "Mankote". The muddy dirt track leads 2km toward the shoreline and to the **Man Kòtè Mangrove**, a primary breeding ground for marine life. The swamp comprises red, white and black mangrove trees, which serve as a protected feeding ground for bird and marine life such as egrets, herons, conch and juvenile fish, as well as buffering the land from sea swells. The ecologically sensitive swamps are dense, and the only bit of Man Kòtè that you can visit is a thin **beach** hugged by palms and sea grape trees. Though it's littered with beer cans, picnic remains and ashes from cooking fires (and not a very pleasant spot to swim), the beach is nicely secluded and is slated for upgrading by the National Trust.

A few minutes further along the coastal highway is the roadside Savannes Bay and the **Savannes Bay Nature Reserve**, marked by a small sign. The reserve is basically a large mangrove swamp surrounding a pretty bay enclosed by **Saltibus Point** to the north and **Burgot Point** to the south; the small **Scorpion Island** sits at the north end of the cove. Amerindians are believed to have settled in the area, and archeological digs have been undertaken at the north and south of the bay. Sheltered by an outlying **reef**, Savannes Bay forms a protected **breeding area** for spiny lobsters, conch and numerous species of fish, and it's a prime fishing spot. Though there are no walking trails or organized activities in the area, fishermen selling their catch at the small market on the highway might be persuaded to take you on a trip around the bay to see the swamp from a different perspective.

POINTE SABLE NATIONAL PARK

The east

Churned up by the Caribbean trade winds, the pounding waters of the Atlantic have carved out a rough and jagged east coast for St Lucia. Characterized by lively surf smashing against rocky, cliff-lined shores and a verdant blanket of banana plants, the area provides a visual as well as atmospheric contrast to the more populated and more touristed north and west of the island.

The **southern** stretch of the east coast is much easier to assess than the northern section of this region, with a constant stream of buses and taxis travelling between Vieux Fort and the capital making it relatively simple to get around. But despite its accessibility, and despite being just a short drive from Hewanorra International Airport where most visitors touch down, the area is often bypassed – seen by many only fleetingly from the window of a bus on its way to the more conventionally tourist-friendly resorts of the northwest coast. There is, however, quite a bit to explore in the area. The appealing village of **Micoud** – one of only two sizeable settlements in eastern St Lucia, just 10km from Vieux Fort – surrounds a diminutive harbour and is known for a couple of lively annual festivals. North of the town, the coastal highway swings past little villages such as Mon Repose; from here, a quick trip into the lush interior brings you to the engaging and vibrant **Mamiku**

Gardens. Back on the coast and just north of Mon Repose, sheltered **Praslin Bay** boasts one of the southeast's few safe swimming beaches – each weekend the sand is crowded with mostly St Lucian beach devotees. At the northern end of the bay, the **Fregate Islands Nature Reserve**, a nesting area for the magnificent frigate bird, can be visited on a guided walking tour, and the **Eastern Nature Trail** makes for a spectacular coastal hike.

Smack in the middle of the eastern coastline, **Dennery** is the only other sizeable town in this part of the island besides Micoud. This fishing and farming stronghold, perhaps best visited on Saturday to coincide with the great fish fry, is the last port of call before the coastal highway strikes inland toward Castries. Nearby, the lovely **Sault Falls** provide a nice spot for a picnic or a swim. North of Dennery, the landscape is distinguished by undramatic, low-lying hills to the west and a decided lack of roads. Tarmac dwindles into rough dirt tracks, and you'll need a 4WD to explore. If you can manage to make it in, though, you'll be rewarded with a fine drive through real St Lucian countryside, ending up at the area's finest **beach** at **Grande Anse**, a sweeping stretch of sand where a planned government park and reserve will soon afford protection to the giant **leatherback turtles** that come here to nest.

For details of accommodation in the east,
see p.173; for eating and drinking, see p.195.

Getting there and around

St Lucia's **coastal highway** parallels the eastern shoreline from Vieux Fort to Dennery, where it cuts inland, heading northwest across the island to Castries. The fastest way to travel the 58km between Vieux Fort and the capital, it's also the preferred route for buses and taxis between the two towns. Along the way, east-coast **bus** stops include Micoud, Desruisseaux (in the hills south of Micoud), Mon Repose, Praslin and Dennery, but exploring the coastline by bus is not particularly efficient as schedules are inconsistent from one day to the next. To travel to the west coast, you'll often need to catch a bus to Vieux Fort for connections to Soufrière and north to Castries – this is a time-consuming route, however. **From Castries**, buses to the south coast leave from Manoel Street, and coming **from Vieux Fort**, New Dock Road is the place to catch a bus to Dennery. You'll pay no more than EC$8 for any single journey.

Taxis shuttle up and down the main highway constantly but are easiest to pick up in Vieux Fort, Micoud or the Dennery area. Fares from Vieux Fort are roughly EC$75 to Micoud, EC$85 to Dennery and EC$140 to Castries.

The most practical way to access the coastal stretch north of Dennery, including Grande Anse, is via the Allan Bousquet Highway, which runs inland from Choc Bay (see pp.69–71) and connects to several laborious dirt tracks that meander toward the coast. These demand a 4WD, which can be rented, albeit for a premium (see p.30). Alternatively you can take a trip with one of several tour companies offering excursions in the area (see p.220).

MICOUD

Map 1, G10.

Named in honour of the French Governor de Micoud, who ruled St Lucia from 1768 to 1771, the relatively size-able town of **MICOUD** spreads back from the sheltered **bay** of **Port Micoud**. The suitability of the harbour to fishing, and the ready availability of fresh water from the **Troumassé River**, which borders the town to the south, are the principal factors cited by archeologists as evidence

MICOUD

of intense **Amerindian** presence in the area. Some nine settlements are believed to have existed in the Micoud Quarter, and to have been rapidly abandoned after the arrival of European settlers in the eighteenth century.

Before the coastal highway was completed in recent years, the old east coast road passed straight through Micoud, typical of St Lucian fishing villages in its numerous compact streets lined with a mix of old homes embellished with West Indian fretwork and modern concrete block architecture. Today, the highway passes about a kilometre north of the village, and a sign marks the turnoff.

Aside from the pretty bay, dotted with fishing boats and churches, Micoud is best known as the birthplace of the island's first prime minister, **John Compton**, though there's nothing to commemorate the connection. The town is also renowned as a particularly enthusiastic focal point for two island-wide religious **festivals**, which also take place throughout the island: **La Rose** in August and **La Marguerite** in October. Rooted in the island's syncretic commingling of African and European religious traditions, the festivals celebrate the Roman Catholic saints Rose of Lima and Marguerite Mary Alacoque through religious services, feasts and flower shows as well as costume parades, parties and public performances of traditional songs and dances. Visitors are welcome to observe, or even join in the fun.

MAMIKU GARDENS

Map 1, G9. Daily 9am–5pm. EC$15, EC$20 with tour. ☏455-3729, Ⓦwww.mamiku.com.

A few minutes' drive north of Micoud, the beautiful **Mamiku Gardens** are thought to have been named after the wife of one-time French Governor de Micoud, who owned an estate here from 1767–1817; "Mamiku" is probably a creolized contraction of her title, Madame de Micoud. By 1796, the property had fallen into the hands of the British, who used it as a military post and command centre for engaging the **Brigands**, escaped slaves who roamed the countryside waging war for freedom. In one of the larger skirmishes, the British engaged the Brigands on the estate property; according to the diary of Captain de Marchay, fifteen British soldiers died and twenty were wounded, and the estate home was burned to the ground. Shamed by the decisive defeat and loss of British lives, Captain de Marchay later committed suicide. The estate was eventually abandoned and its buildings left in ruins until the turn of the twentieth century, when it was turned into a commercial banana and tropical flower plantation.

Today, the fifteen-acre gardens are resplendent with brightly coloured exotic blooms, such as hibiscus, ginger and heliconia; tree species include the carambola and gommier (the area's distinctive dugout fishing boats are fashioned from the latter; see opposite). You can explore the gardens via a simple network of short **walking trails**, each with resting spots at suitably beautiful points. One five-minute trail leads to the top of a hill that holds the foundations of the old plantation house and provides extraordinary views of nearby Praslin Bay (see p.131). If you don't stop to admire the scenery, the longest trail will take about twenty minutes to walk. You can pick up a free brochure at the entrance, which has a map, or ask someone to guide you through the trails (EC$5 extra). Though the paths themselves are short, there's a lot to see, and you'll probably spend a couple of hours exploring. There's also a small, friendly café (snacks only) and a gift shop on site.

Mamiku is located on the west side of the highway, between the roadside village of Mon Repose and Praslin Bay. A sign marks the turnoff, from where it's a two-minute drive (or a five-minute walk).

MAMIKU GARDENS

PRASLIN BAY

Map 1, G9.

A 2km cove split in two by a rocky outcrop, the sheltered **Praslin Bay** offers one of the southeast's few opportunities for a safe ocean swim. Blessed with a gentle surf and plenty of shade, the **beach** at Praslin is long and wide, protected by the narrow bay entrance and enclosed by high hills. As this is one of the nicest swimming spots in the area, it's likely to be busy on holidays and weekends, popular as it is with young St Lucians. There's no official place to park, so if you're driving, you'll have to find a space at the side of the highway before following one of several paths leading down a precipitous embankment to the beach. There are no facilities, but a few vendors peddle cold drinks and snacks on the weekends. Toward the middle of the bay is tiny **Praslin Island**, which you can visit with an authorized guide from the St Lucia National Trust (see p.132).

Praslin is also noted for its distinctive **fishing boats**, carved out from whole gommier tree trunks and distinguished by their upturned, pointed bows: there are usually a few moored up at the small pier in the centre of the bay.

Fregate Islands Nature Reserve and Eastern Nature Trail

Map 1, G8. Daily Aug–April 9am–5pm; tours only. EC$55 for Fregate Islands Nature Reserve; EC$10 for Eastern Nature Trail, plus EC$60 guide fee (for up to 15 people).

Occupying the northern section of Praslin Bay, the **Fregate Islands Nature Reserve** is centred around the two tiny **cays** just metres offshore that are named after the seagoing **frigate bird** that nests here between May and July. Glossy jet-black birds with forked tail feathers, male frigates have distinctive red or bright orange throat pouches, which are expanded during mating time to attract females. Also known as the magnificent frigate or the man-o'-war bird, the frigate's two-metre wingspan allows it to remain in soaring and swooping flight for great lengths of time, and it's thought that they even sleep while floating on air currents. Because they lack the oily plumage film that allows other seabirds to shed water and resurface after diving, rather than risk drowning after a plunge into the ocean, frigates feed by skimming the water's surface for fish, or simply by stealing from other birds.

The reserve is also home to several other **bird species**, including herons, yellow-eyed, brown-feathered tremblers and St Lucia orioles, black with orange patches on the belly and underside of the wings. Also occasionally seen on the island is one of St Lucia's larger **snakes**, a dark tan boa constrictor that's locally known as *tête chien* and often attains a length of four metres. Tan with orange, diamond-shaped markings, the poisonous *fer de lance* snake is also found in isolated sections of the east coast, but you're extremely unlikely to see these shy creatures. St Lucia's indigenous lizard, the *zandoli tè* (see p.140), can now also be found on these islands.

You're not allowed onto the islands themselves, but the reserve can be explored on the mainland section via an easy 1.5km **walking trail** (guided walks only). The trail loops through a changing landscape of thick vegetation to dry spots of low-lying bushes and cacti, passing a **waterfall** that flows in the rainy season, a mangrove swamp and an observation point overlooking the Fregate Islands before returning to base. The reserve is marked by a sign in front of a small car park on the ocean side of the highway. However, when you get there, you'll probably find the entrance gated and locked – the Fregates are maintained by the **St Lucia National Trust** (call ahead for a visit; ☎452-5005) and no one is allowed in without one of their authorized guides, who will conduct tours along the trails for two or more people (price included in the entrance fee). If you do find the gates unlocked you can look around the **interpretive centre**, a wooden hut in the car park, which has maps and illustrations of wildlife found in the reserve. Despite the inconveniences, a tour is well worth the time it takes to set it up. At extra cost, the National Trust can also arrange transportation from Castries, lunch and a boat tour to the unoccupied **Praslin Island** in the centre of Praslin Bay (see p.131).

A few minutes north of the interpretative centre, along the main road, lies the start of the **Eastern Nature Trail**. This five-and-a-half-kilometre guided hike stretches north from Praslin Bay towards Dennery through some stunning wilderness coastline, and often affords sightings of as many as 38 species of bird, including the magnificent frigate. Ask at the interpretative centre for a guide, or contact the St Lucia National Trust (see opposite). Details can also be found at ⊛www.slunatrust.org/naturetrail.htm.

DENNERY

Map 1, G7.

Once known as Anse Canot, and later as Le Grand Mouyaba, **DENNERY** was given its current name by the French, following a 1768 visit to the town by then-governor of the Windward Islands, Count D'Ennery. The village extends back from a deep and protected **bay**, with uninhabited **Dennery Island** at its northern tip. A major export centre for agricultural produce throughout the nineteenth century, Dennery remains a farming community today, and – since the addition of the large, Japanese-funded Daito Complex and Pier processing facility – it's also one of St Lucia's busiest **fishing** centres.

The **town** itself is a jumble of compact streets with a few bars but nothing much in the way of tourist sights, though on Saturday nights the place comes alive with the **fish fry**

DENNERY

on the seafront. A pleasant, low-key and mainly local affair, it's much less developed than the overpriced affairs at Anse La Raye and Gros Islet, and much less touristy too. The looming white- and rust-coloured **St Peter's Roman Catholic Church** sits a block from the water; built from stone and mortar between 1789 and 1841, the church is one of the oldest on the island.

Sault Falls

Map 1, G7

The **Sault Falls** (also known as the Errard Falls and the Dennery Falls) are among the tallest and prettiest on the island, and have a large swimming pool below and pleasant picnic area nearby. You need a 4WD to reach them, but the route is easy. Take the main road south out of Dennery – as you leave you will see a cream-coloured concrete bus shelter. Take the right turn directly opposite this shelter, continuing past the Belle Fashions and furniture making factories until you reach the falls. Sunlink (☎452-8232) also provides a Sault Falls tour.

GRANDE ANSE

Map 1, G4.

Around 10km north of Dennery, the wide, windswept **Grande Anse beach** boasts more than 2km of blonde sand set against a backdrop of cliffs and hills covered with dry vegetation. Once part of a plantation estate, the bay sits in the middle of an area slated to become a new **national park** comprising several other nearby beaches, such as **Petite Anse** to the north and **Anse Louvet** to the south. Amerindian **petroglyphs** and artefacts have been found within the proposed park area at Petite Anse, Grande Anse, Tortue Point and Anse Pouvert, and the area is rich with historical significance.

The **beach** itself is inviting and often devoid of visitors, but as strong winds usually churn up a rough surf, swimming can be risky and many people have died through recklessness here. The main attraction of Grand Anse, though, is the annual visit of sea turtles. The bay is the primary St Lucian nesting spot for endangered **leatherback turtles**, which also lay their eggs at Fond D'Or, the next bay north of Dennery. While the more common (but still protected in St Lucian waters) hawksbill and green back turtles nest at a number of beaches around the island, it's the endangered leatherbacks that prefer to make their annual journey to Grande Anse's inviting sands to burrow out egg-laying chambers – in 1997, a record figure of 116 females were counted here. During the leatherback egg-laying season, roughly March through July, volunteers head out to Grande Anse to monitor nesting females and protect the turtles and their eggs from predators and human poachers. Periodic upgrades of the roads to Grande Anse have led to an increase in the latter, while the excavation of large quantities of sand for use in building work has threatened both the turtles' habitat and the beauty of the beach. For now, though, leatherbacks are still coming to Grande Anse, and you can witness them nesting for yourself by joining one of the **turtle watches** (see overleaf).

Despite the regrading, most of the roads to Grande Anse remain dirt and gravel tracks that become impassable after rains. A sedan car might make it, but a 4WD is a safer bet, and it's a good idea to ask locals about current conditions. Access is most often easiest from the west coast at Choc Bay (see pp.69–71), via the paved Allan Bousquet Highway. At Babonneau, turn off onto the gravel and dirt track that leads to the village of Desbarra, from where a single track leads down to Grande Anse. The eleven-kilometre ride from Choc Bay can take up to an hour and a half.

THE LEATHERBACK TURTLE

The rarest – and the largest – of the sea turtles that frequent Caribbean waters is the **leatherback** (*Dermochelys coriacea*), which has a shell as long as 1.5m and a body weight of up to 680kg; a male weighing in at 1144kg is the biggest specimen on record.

Named for their triangular **carapace** or shell, which is covered by a layer of leathery brown and black skin rather than the hard scales of other species, leatherback turtles have changed little in their 65 million years of existence. However, they now face **extinction**: leatherbacks are still hunted by humans, and ocean pollution and accidental entrapment in fishing nets kill thousands. Furthermore, their laying beaches are being transformed into tourist resorts or diminished by sand mining, and as their main food is **jellyfish**, they often mistake floating plastic waste for food – the immense male mentioned above was found with 24 plastic bags in his intestines.

Nesting females are among the most implacable mothers on earth, leaving the ocean every two to six years only to lay eggs. Under the cover of night, they lumber up the sand and burrow the hole into which they lay around eighty eggs before returning to the sea for about ten days. Females will go through this process up to a dozen times during a laying period, depositing as many as eight hundred eggs during the March to July season. These incubate for as long as three months and produce fully functional **hatchlings**, which emerge at night and paw their way to the surf. Only an average one in a thousand baby leatherbacks survives the six years it takes to reach maturity.

Turtle watch

In conjunction with the Department of Fisheries, Heritage Tours organizes an annual programme of eco-sensitive

turtle watches, known as the Debarras Turtlewatch, which allow visitors to experience the stirring spectacle of leatherback turtles laying their eggs. The all-night watches take place daily in leatherback breeding season (March through July) and cost US$65, which covers transport from your hotel, tent expenses, dinner, breakfast, sleeping mats and a T-shirt; you'll have to bring your own flashlight, toilet paper and warm clothing, as nights can be cool and breezy. Once at the beach, you settle into a rustic tent village and take turns patrolling the beach. Whenever a turtle is spotted, you'll be called to have a look. The watches are becoming very popular, so to ensure a place, it's best to contact Heritage Tours well in advance (PO Box GM868, Castries, St Lucia, WI; ⊤451-6620 or 451-6967, ⊛www.heritagetoursstlucia.com.

The interior forest reserves

Stretching across the island's central interior, the vast and eerily serene **St Lucia Forest Reserve** comprises the 19,000 acres of rainforest and dry forest maintained by the government's forestry department. The entire reserve is divided into smaller, loosely demarcated sub-regions, most still referred to by the names given in the early colonial days when forest trails were the shortest route between St Lucia's east and west coasts. These days, though, most people who venture in do so for pleasure rather than necessity. Arrestingly beautiful, and full of exotic flora and fauna, the forests – uninhabited by humans – offer an absorbing alternative to the sun-and-beach culture of coastal resorts.

Essentially, the interior reserves have been created to protect the island's last portions of unfarmed virgin forest and the often-rare animals and birds that inhabit them, but the area is also used for recreation and many of the reserve's **hiking trails** have been opened up to the public. Of these, the easiest is probably the **Union Nature Trail** near Babonneau (see p.142) in the northwest. Though it isn't actually in the reserve proper, it's a pleasant stroll, and the small, on-site **zoo** provides an overview of local wildlife. Another unchallenging walk, both in terms of access and level of difficulty, is the **Barre de L'Isle Trail**, which begins alongside the Castries–Dennery highway and leads for about 2km along the north–south ridge that bisects this section of the island. The three-and-a-half hour guided walk through the thick **Edmund Forest Reserve** ends up near Morne Gimie – the island's highest peak at 950 metres – in the southwest, and the area also contains the 4km **Enbas Saut Falls Trail** featuring a couple of spectacular swimmable waterfalls. From Mahaut, just inland from Micoud over on the eastern side of the island, the four-kilometre **Des Cartiers Rainforest Trail** provides a succinct introduction to tropical rainforests.

While the most popular of the interior hikes are the Barre de L'Isle, Edmund Reserve and Des Cartiers Rainforest trails, even these are unlikely to be teeming with tourists – hiking is not high up on many people's Caribbean itineraries, and unless you go with a commercial tour (see below), you'll most likely have St Lucia's hiking trails entirely to yourself.

Hiking practicalities

A division of the awkwardly named Ministry of Agriculture, Lands, Forestry, Fisheries and Environment, the **Forestry and Lands Department** (☎450-2231 or 450-207, ⓦwww.slumaffe.org) maintains St Lucia's protected forest reserves and all of the hiking trails within them. The division also determines public access (some parts of the interior are restricted) and provides trained **hiking guides**. A flat fee of EC$25 covers access to a single trail as well as the services of a guide, vital for exploring ecologically sensitive and challenging hikes such as Morne Gimie

COMMON FOREST FLORA AND FAUNA

The **topography** of the forest reserve is immensely varied, ranging from relatively flat plateaux to steep summits. The peaks and valleys of the central mountains are covered by rich, green woodlands, and the high mountain altitudes create nourishing rain and mist, generating prolific semi-rainforest woodlands and primordial "montane" **rainforests**. These nearly 20,000 acres of rainforest, which comprise about thirteen percent of St Lucia's total landmass, host mammoth trees whose mossy branches groan with epiphytic bromeliads, orchids and even mushrooms, and also feature giant ferns, twisting lianas and a plethora of other plant and tree species.

Making their homes among the reserve's trees – which include the indigenous and ubiquitous **gommier** and **chatagnier** varieties – are numerous species of **birds**, of which the most famous is the **St Lucia parrot** or *jacquot* (*Amazona versicolor*), recognizable by the brilliant blue feathers on its head, green wings, yellow tail and red spot at its breast. In the past,

or the Edmund Reserve cross-island walk. At extra cost, the forestry department can also arrange **transport** to the trails, but travel arrangements might depend upon a minimum number of people on the walk; tours are often subcontracted to commercial companies, which means you'll be traipsing along a quiet rainforest trail with twenty other people and are unlikely to get the most out of the experience. As the forestry department is understaffed (ranger stations at the start of the trails are sometimes un-manned) and, at times, poorly organized, you should always call a few days in advance to arrange guides or transport, and it's also well worth clarifying the details of forestry department transport before you book.

If you do want to hike, remember that although you're in

the *jacquot* was often hunted for its feathers, and numbers had reached a low of 150 by the late 1970s. Conservation programmes were initiated in 1978, and today, there are thought to be more than 350 *jacquot* living in the forest reserve. Some of the other birds found here are the **white-breasted thrasher**, the **St Lucia oriole** and the **St Lucia peewee**.

Though the numbers have been reduced by hunting, the most common **mammals** in the forests include the shy **agouti**, a rabbit-sized rodent with muscular hind legs, and the cat-sized **manicou**, an opossum with a long snout and a rat-like tail. Other animals include rats, mice and the **mongoose**, a ferret-like creature that feeds on smaller rodents, snakes and domestic fowl. **Reptiles** include the endemic St Lucia **tree lizard** and the **pygmy gecko**, tiny and light green; dark brown and black with a row of spiny protrusions along the neck, the prehistoric-looking **iguana** grows to as long as 2m and is found in trees, where it feeds on leaves and fruits.

the mountains, it will be hot, so you should bring sunscreen and a hat as well as plenty of drinking water and some snacks. Light clothing is fine and sturdy footwear is a must for all hikes. During the rainy season (see p.3), wet-weather gear is a good idea.

Getting to the trails

Unless you have your own vehicle or elect to arrange your **transport** with the forestry department or go with Castries-based commercial **tour companies** such as Jungle Tours (℡450-0434, ⓦwww.jungletoursstlucia.com) or Sunlink (℡452-8232 or 456-9127, ⓦwww.sunlinktours.com), travelling to the interior forests can be tricky. Public transport is limited, but you can reach some trails by taking an inland **bus** (EC$5 or less) from Castries. Services run directly to the start of the Union and Barre de L'Isle walks, but for the other hikes listed in this chapter, you'll have to take a bus to the nearest town and walk to the start of the trail, often a few kilometres away; see individual hikes for details. If you decide to opt for a **taxi**, make arrangements to be collected at an appointed hour, as you're unlikely to find drivers cruising for fares in the mountains. Renting a **car** is probably the easiest option, and regular sedan vehicles will get you to the start of all of the trails covered here.

UNION NATURE TRAIL

Map 1, E4. Daily 8am–4.30pm. EC$25.

The forestry department's field headquarters – about half an hour's drive from Castries – is the starting point for the short, easy **Union Nature Trail**, and the complex also contains a herb garden, a small **zoo** and an **interpretive centre** with information on endangered indigenous species, vegetation zones and the like. Usually inside the main office building, rangers are on site every day between 11.30am and 3pm to give **tours** of the centre and the walking trails, but you're free to amble about by yourself during opening hours.

The centre's tiny and tidy **zoo** houses some fifty animals common to St Lucia and the Caribbean, but it's a sad affair, with animals pacing, jabbering and generally looking distressed. Inmates include **vervet monkeys**, light grey in colour with a dark facial "mask", several **boa constrictors**, a couple of **agoutis** and birds such as **macaws**, orange-winged **parrots** and the island's national bird, the **St Lucia parrot** or *jacquot*; as these are rarely seen in the wild, this might be your best opportunity to view a *jacquot* up close, albeit a rather confused and dishevelled specimen.

The **Union Nature Trail** begins just to the left of the rangers' office and loops through dry forest, taking about an hour if you don't make too many stops. At only 1.6km, it's an easy stroll, with gentle slopes rising to 100m and occasional hillocks to scramble, but it's simple to follow and you don't need a guide. Free **pamphlets** that explain some of the flora along the trail (and in the medicinal garden – see below) are available from the rangers, and common trees such as almond, glory cedar, gommier and calabash are labelled with plaques.

You might want some expert ranger input when walking the shorter path just behind the office, which winds through a small **medicinal garden** where rangers grow herbs used in traditional cures. The *wallwort* leaf, for example, is boiled with milk and imbibed for colds and fever, and the *kasialata* leaf can be rubbed on the skin to stop itching.

To get to the interpretive centre, head north along the Castries–Gros Islet Highway for about ten minutes before turning inland toward Babonneau along the signposted Allan Bousquet Highway. There are no signs to signify that you've reached Union, but after a winding 2.5km, you'll see a large fence to the right, which protects the station's agricultural propagation field; turn right at its end to reach the centre. **Buses** travelling the Allan Bousquet Highway leave from Jeremie Street in Castries and will drop you at the turnoff for the station, but getting back can be more of a problem; services are infrequent, and you'll probably end up walking back to the Castries–Gros Islet Highway.

BARRE DE L'ISLE TRAIL

Map 1, E7-E8. Mon–Fri 8.30am–4.30pm. EC$25.

Literally translated as "island ridge", the **Barre de L'Isle Trail** meanders along the north–south ridge that bisects the Central Forest Reserve. It's a worthwhile morning or

BARRE DE L'ISLE TRAIL

afternoon adventure and provides a good insight into St Lucia's richly diverse topography and mountain flora and fauna, and affords some expansive vistas.

The **signposted start** of the Barre de L'Isle Trail strikes into the forest directly from the central Castries–Dennery highway, a twenty- to thirty-minute drive or bus journey from downtown Castries; buses leave from Manoel Street – tell the driver where you're heading, as he'll know where to drop you. Once you've cleared Morne Fortune and the Cul de Sac Valley, rainforest vegetation becomes evident: the roadside is swathed with bamboo, elephant ferns and dark, towering trees. Opposite the sign marking the start of the trail is a gravel road leading up a hillock to the **rangers' hut**, where you pay your entrance fee and can hire a guide. The hut is usually staffed, but an escort isn't strictly necessary for this easy-to-follow walk; a guide will, however, be able to identify bird species as well as trees and plants along the trail, and you might have a better time if you take someone along.

Extending about 2km into the forest (you retrace your steps on the way back), the trail is a steep but relatively undemanding two-hour hike that alternates between cool, thick forests where the canopies of towering trees block out most of the sunlight, and wide-open hilltops that provide remarkable views of the coast and of Central Reserve mountain ranges, including Morne Gimie to the south. The 438-metre Mount La Combe lies near to the start of the trail, and you can extend your hike by another couple of hours by electing to climb it. As you'd expect, the mountain trail is steep in places, but the reward for your effort is panoramic views that stretch south, east and west.

EDMUND FOREST RESERVE

Map 1, D10. Daily 8am–4pm. EC$25 per trail.

The only way to explore the **Edmund Forest Reserve**,

which spreads over the southwestern interior, is on a somewhat strenuous ten-kilometre, three-and-a-half-hour guided hike. Traversing the heart of the island to the open western plains, the trail allows wonderful views along the way, including a spectacular sighting of **Morne Gimie**. It starts from the main access road to the rainforest, about ten minutes' walk beyond the ranger station; you might want to hire a guide here (see p.146). Starting **early** is advisable: you'll benefit from the cool of the morning, and it's a good idea to allow plenty of time for stops.

The trail, which is mostly over flat terrain, with some small streams and crevices spanned by footbridges, provides lots of **birdwatching** opportunities – keep your eyes open for the rare *jacquot* (see box on p.140), as well as orioles, white-breasted thrashers and various hummingbirds. For much of the time, you're in the shadow of Morne Gimie, while in some spots, the panoramas of the mountains are vast.

Several **alternative routes** branch off from the main Edmund Trail, some leading toward the south and others to Morne Gimie. If you want to tackle the latter, you'll need a specialist guide, which can be arranged through the ranger station. However, it's an arduous and time-consuming hike that isn't often attempted.

The eight-kilometre drive to the Edmund Reserve will take about an hour from the west coast, and if it hasn't rained recently you should be able to make it in a regular rental car. From Soufrière, take the inland road to Fond St Jacques, a tiny rural community (don't expect to be able to stock up on food and drink here) and the last village before the road becomes little more than a track leading only to the rainforest. Buses from Soufrière go only as far as here, and if you've travelled in on public transport, you'll have to walk the remaining 5km to the start of the trail.

The spur road to the trail turns left off the main road by a zinc-roofed cement bus stop in the centre of the village.

After a few minutes, the lush forest flora becomes noticeable: looming, bromeliad-bedecked trees filter the sunlight, while elephant ferns interspersed with broad-leafed dasheen plants planted by farmers smother the side of the road. To the north, the peak of Morne Gimie is occasionally visible through breaks in the trees, and there is a noticeable increase in humidity.

After a twenty- to thirty-minute drive, depending on the condition of the road, a wooden forestry department **ranger station** is the first indication that you're in the reserve itself and at the start of the trail; it's usually staffed by forestry guides and officers who'll collect your entrance fee. Hiking with a **guide** is highly recommended; side trails branch off the main route and it is easy to get lost. You may be able to hire a guide at the ranger station, but to be on the safe side, call the forestry department in Castries (☎450-2231) a few days before you plan to hike. If you elect to walk the whole trail, you'll need to arrange for someone to drop you at the start and collect you at the trail end at Mahaut. Alternatively, if you've got your own transport, you can simply park at the trailhead and turn back when you're ready.

Enbas Saut Falls Trail

Map 1, D10.

To the immediate left of the ranger station at the Edmund Forest Reserve is a sign marking the start of the **Enbas Saut Falls Trail**, a moderate to strenuous four-kilometre loop trail cut into the wilderness, allowing good opportunities to see St Lucia's native flora and fauna (including the *jacquot*) and leading to a couple of spectacular falls, with clean, deep pools in which you can swim. You can walk the trail alone or with a guide; ask at the ranger station for further information.

DES CARTIERS RAINFOREST

Map 1, E10. Daily 8am–4pm. EC$25.

The **Des Cartiers Rainforest** is handy for those staying in the southern half of the island, with an easy four-kilometre **trail** providing a good introduction to St Lucia's interior riches and saving visitors the hassle of trekking in to less accessible parts of the reserve. The hike follows old military roads laid by the French during World War II; it's well marked and a guide isn't necessary. From the reserve, you can also link up with the Edmund Reserve Trail, which threads through the centre of the island toward the west coast (see p.145); however, it's a rigorous four-hour trek, and a guide is essential.

The Des Cartiers Rainforest lies some ten kilometres into the mountains from the east coast highway, and the Des Cartiers Trail begins at a small, sporadically staffed forestry department **interpretive centre**, where you pay your entrance fee and can peruse the displays on rainforest plant species; adjacent are toilets and a roofed picnic hut. More than 300m above sea level throughout, the trail is a mostly flat, looping hike that skirts the **Canelles River** and brings you back to the ranger station in about two hours. There are several marked lookout spots, said to be haunts of the *jacquot*, and sweeping views can be had of the south and east coasts from a couple of higher elevation points. At the northern stage of the loop, you'll find the marked turnoff for the Edmund Forest Reserve Trail.

The primary route into the Des Cartiers Rainforest is a signposted turnoff a minute or so north of the east coast village of Micoud (see p.128). The road is in good condition, passing through the tiny settlement of Anbre and running parallel to a small branch of the Canelles River. Local people swim in the water, but as it's polluted, taking a dip is not really advisable. From the coast, it's a thirty-minute drive to the boundary of the reserve. **Buses** into the eastern interior are extremely infrequent, and if you don't have a rental car, you're best off hiring a **taxi** if you want to walk the Des Cartiers Trail. You'll pay about EC$70 one-way from Vieux Fort, and you should arrange for the driver to wait or come back and collect you.

LISTINGS

Accommodation

Tourist facilities on St Lucia have improved greatly over the last two decades, and accommodation runs the full range, from spa and sushi all-inclusives and medium-sized family hotels to inexpensive local bed and breakfasts and guesthouses and even a campsite. The majority of establishments are moderately sized and priced, but large resorts and luxury exclusionist locales are becoming increasingly common – a source of some local contention and dismay – though the island is still thankfully not as dominated by all-inclusives as many Caribbean islands

Most of the island's accommodation is located along the **west coast**, where the calm waters lend themselves to conventional resort activities. North of Castries, the stretch of coast from **Vigie Beach** to **Cap Estate**, including the heavily visited areas of **Rodney Bay** and **Gros Islet**, is known as the "Golden Mile" – here you'll find some of St Lucia's best beaches and the greatest concentration of accommodation. South of Castries, another crop of hotels springs up at the secluded and quiet **Marigot Bay**, less than 8km from the capital. There's a little tourist buzz here, but it remains a tranquil bay dotted with moored yachts and a handful of small hotels and restaurants. In the southwest, the historic town of **Soufrière** now hosts several exclusive resorts as well as smaller, more economical hotels and

ACCOMMODATION PRICE CODES

All accommodation listed in this guide has been price-graded according to the rate charged for the cheapest double or twin room during high season (mid-Dec to mid-April). In the low season rates can be reduced by up to forty percent, and it's not unusual to get smaller discounts in the quieter spring and autumn months at either end of the high season.

❶ up to US$30
❷ US$30–70
❸ US$70–110
❹ US$110–150

❺ US$150–190
❻ US$190–230
❼ US$230 and above

guesthouses. Further south at **Vieux Fort**, the relatively few hotels tend to be functional rather than flamboyant, servicing nearby Hewanorra International Airport. With fewer beaches and an infrastructure still based on fishing and farming, the **southeast coast** offers limited but worthwhile accommodation choices, convenient for excursions into the interior forest reserves. Note that all accommodation reviewed in this chapter is cross-referenced to the maps at the back of the book.

When **booking** accommodation, it's important to bear in mind that St Lucian hotels generally levy a ten percent **service charge** and an eight percent **government tax**, which are either included in quoted rates or tacked on to the final bill at the end of your stay. All-inclusive hotels include all taxes and service charges in their rates, as do most small guesthouses (though some disregard them entirely). Medium-sized hotels can go either way. The prices quoted in this guide are exclusive of that eighteen percent tax.

It's worth knowing that **toll-free** hotel booking numbers generally connect you to an outside reservation service rather than the hotel itself. You may get a more favourable rate, as well as more accurate and up-to-date information about airport transfers, amenities, special packages and promotional rates by calling individual properties direct.

Tourist offices on the island and abroad (see pp.21–22) will send out brochures and comprehensive lists of approved accommodation, as will the **St Lucia Hotel and Tourism Association**, PO Box 545, Castries, St Lucia, WI (℡ 452-5978 or 1-888-744-2772, ℻ 452-7967, ⓦ www.stluciatravel .com.lc), and the **Inns of St Lucia**, 20 Bridge St, Castries, St Lucia, W1 (℡ 452-4599, ℻ 452-5428, ⓦ www.st-lucia .com/lcacc01.htm#inns), a marketing group representing about three dozen small properties offering simple, comfortable and moderately priced accommodation.

All-inclusives

A concept pioneered by the *SuperClubs* and *Sandals* chains of Jamaica (*Sandals* has two resorts on St Lucia with talk of a possible third in the next few years), **all-inclusives** are precisely what the name implies: resorts where your room, all meals, snacks, drinks, sports, amenities and tips are included in the price. You'll usually only have to pay for things like laundry, telephone and internet use and certain sports such as scuba diving.

The advantage of all-inclusives is the clarity of exchange. You needn't be bothered by tipping, arguing over who pays for dinner or secreting loose change in your sandals on the beach. The disadvantage is one of local economics and attitude. As everything is already paid for, there's little incentive to leave the resort, which of course antagonizes the local restaurateurs, bar owners and watersports operators, who rely on tourism to make a living. For the most part, the local community (except for employees and suppliers) sees few monetary benefits from their all-inclusive resort neighbours. Quite apart from that, you have to ask yourself

ACCOMMODATION

if a trip where you feel financially compelled to eat, drink and socialize in the same few acres is right for you. Though most resorts do offer and indeed encourage day trips to other parts of the island – for a hefty fee – what seems like ease and facility can soon feel claustrophobic. Still, all-inclusive resorts seem to enjoy a booming business, and their offers can be tempting, particularly when combined with airfare and ground transport. It's important to read the small print before booking to check which activities are included; and remember that the rate quoted will often be for one person based on double occupancy rather than per room. For more details on packages, see pp.7,11,14.

Renting a villa

Essentially multi-bedroom houses for rent, **villas** are scattered throughout the island and are often the most convenient and inexpensive option for families, larger groups and those who want to get away from the tourist stream. Rates often include maid and cooking services, rental cars and other amenities; split several ways, a villa can work out to be extremely cost-effective. Count on spending US$700–4000 per week in high season.

For **rentals**, contact Tropical Villas, PO Box 189, Castries, St Lucia, WI (℡452-8240, Ⓕ452-8089, Ⓦwww.tropicalvillas .net); Island Link Villa Service, PO Box 370, Castries, St Lucia, WI (℡453-6341, Ⓕ453-6303); or Top O' The Morne, PO Box 376, Castries (℡452-3603, Ⓕ453-1433).

Camping

Camping has yet to catch on in the Caribbean, and there's only one campground on St Lucia, at **Anse la Liberté**, south of Anse la Raye. Maintained by the National Trust (℡459-4540, 453-7656 or 454-5014, Ⓕ453-2791, Ⓦwww.slunatrust.org/ans_la_liberte.htm), it's near to a small, somewhat rocky beach, and is perfect if

you want to get away from it all. Facilities include perma-
nent tents on wooden platforms, bare sites, barbecue
grills, a communal, solar-powered pavilion, showers and
toilets, all set in four miles of hiking trails. Be sure to call
ahead and check what's available. For two people sharing,
prices are: bare sites EC$50, plain tent EC$75, elevated
platforms EC$100.

The government allows some camping in selected areas
of the interior **forest reserves** (covered in Chapter 6).
There is no system as such, but permission is granted on a
case-by-case basis by the Forestry and Lands Division,
Environmental Education Unit, Ministry of Agriculture,
Castries (T 450-2231). It's free to camp at present, but the
Forestry Division has indicated that payment will be
required in the future. Keep in mind that you have to hike
in (and out) carrying all your provisions and equipment. If
you strike out without permission, you'll make the Forestry
Division unhappy to the point of possible prosecution;
additionally, certain sections of the forest are not suitable for
camping; if you are hurt or in trouble out there, no one
will know where you are.

It's also highly inadvisable to pitch a tent on the beach,
unless you're with an organized group such as the Grande
Anse turtle watch (see p.136). As well as being potentially
dangerous – you are exposed to theft and other crime – you
might well be camping illegally on private land.

CASTRIES AND AROUND

Unless you have a yearning for busy streets and the noise
and smell of slow-moving traffic, there's no compelling reason to stay in **downtown Castries**, and you'll find that
most of the hotels are more pleasantly located on the harbour or bays immediately north and south of town; these
also have the advantage of easy access to city transport.

The **hills** surrounding the capital hold several small properties, distinguished by their reasonable rates and well-regarded restaurants. You won't be on a beach, but you'll have the benefit of refreshing breezes, not to mention views of the harbour, town and neighbouring islands. North of downtown, **Vigie Peninsula** has several excellent restaurants as well as accommodation used mostly by businesspeople. Along the Castries–Gros Islet Highway north of Castries, a wide range of resorts, from all-inclusives to smaller hotels and guesthouses, sit on or close by the beaches of **Choc Bay**. Just north of here, the sheltered Labrellotte Bay and Bois d'Orange hills host several of the island's most popular hotels. Public transport to all spots in and around Castries is plentiful and inexpensive.

Auberge Seraphine
Map 3, C6. Vieille Bay, Pointe Seraphine ⓣ 453-2073, ⓕ 452-7001, ⓦ www.aubergeseraphine .com.
Set on a small, green inlet on the west side of Pointe Seraphine and favoured by business travellers for its easy access to downtown Castries. Each of the 24 spacious and modern upscale rooms have a porch, a/c, cable TV and hair dryer. There's a patio with pool and sun deck above the restaurant. ❸

Bon Appetit
Map 3, B8. Morne Road, Morne Fortune ⓣ 452-2757.

The best aspect of this four-room guesthouse in the hills is its small but highly regarded French/West Indian restaurant (see p.181). The rooms are basic, clean and secure, each with private bath, TV and fan; rates include breakfast. ❷

Cara Suites Hotel
Map 3, D6. La Pansee ⓣ 452-4767, ⓕ 435-1999, ⓦ www .carahotels.com.
High on a hill on the east side of Castries, and just half a mile from the city centre, this modern business-oriented hotel has 54 rooms with a/c, cable TV and balconies, as

well as a pool and decent restaurant. Functional rather than romantic, it's clean and well-equipped. ❸

E's Serenity Lodge

Map 3, F4. Sunny Acres ⓣ452-1987, ⓕ451-6019. Twelve charming rooms, some en suite, make up this handsome, modern guesthouse set in a well-manicured garden with verandah and large balcony. Close to shopping, restaurants and beaches, but tucked away from the busy main road. ❷

East Winds Inn

Map 3, F2. Labrellotte Bay ⓣ452-8212, ⓕ452-9941, ⓦwww.eastwinds.com. Pretty meets palatial in this understated, peaceful all-inclusive. Rooms are spacious and well appointed, with plunge showers and mini fridges; the beach is private and the pool sizeable. There are no staff variety shows here, nor group activities; what sets *East Winds* above the rest are the rooms, the restaurant and the handsome gardens. ❼

Golden Arrow Inn

Map 3, G1. Marisule ⓣ450-1832, ⓕ450-2329, ⓔcopincopinestours@candw.lc. Set on the beach side of the Castries–Gros Islet Highway, but not on the water, these fifteen rooms are rudimentary, with en-suite baths and fans. The favourable location and reasonable rates make up for the lack of a restaurant or pool. ❷

Green Parrot Inn

Map 3, B8. Morne Fortune ⓣ452-3399 or 452-3167, ⓕ453-2272. Slightly tatty and infused with the air of a former hot spot, this 55-room inn in the hills south of Castries offers a chance to wallow in the coolish breezes drifting up the hills. The restaurant's West Indian cuisine is a real draw, as is its alfresco seating with views of Castries below (see p.181). There's a pool, and the hotel provides complimentary transport to local beaches. ❹

Rendezvous Hotel

Map 3, D5. Malabar Beach, Vigie ⓣ452-4211 or 1-800/544-

2883 (US), ⓕ 452-7419,
ⓦ www.rendezvous.com.lc.
Billing itself as "the escape for
romantics", this sprawling
seven-acre, mixed-sex-
couples-only all-inclusive on
Malabar Beach has tons of
watersports and amenities,
including hot tubs, two pools,
tennis, fitness rooms, scuba
diving, golf and nightly
entertainment as well as a
couple of restaurants and bars.
The vast rooms are luxurious
and designed with honey-
mooners in mind, though the
"concept" may prove too
formulaic for some. ❼

Sandals Halcyon and Sandals St Lucia Golf Resort and Spa

Halcyon: **Map 3, F4**. Choc Bay
ⓣ 453-0222 or 1-800/726-3247
(US), ⓕ 451-8453.
St Lucia: **Map 3, A7**. La Toc
Bay ⓣ 452-3081 or 1-800/726-
3247 (US), ⓕ 452-1012,
ⓦ www.sandals.com.
The beaches at these two
Sandals resorts are wide with
calm water, and the all-
inclusive *Sandals* formula for
success – generic island fun –
is no different here than in

Jamaica, where the chain
originated and gained its
reputation for excellent food,
extensive sports facilities and
luxury rooms. *Sandals St
Lucia* is the larger of the two,
with a nine-hole golf course
and spa, but guests at either
resort can access the beaches,
nine restaurants and amenities
of both via an hourly shuttle.
Note, however, that *Sandals* is
dedicated to the maintenance
of the happily married
heterosexual status quo, so no
same-sex couples, no kids and
no singles allowed. ❼

Seascape

Map 3, F2. Bon Air, Marisule
ⓣ 450-1645, ⓕ 452-7967,
ⓦ www.seascape-stlucia.com.
Three wonderful, if basic,
self-contained wooden
cottages with balconies, set in
acres of beautiful gardens and
sweeping down to a secluded
beach below. The well-
ventilated rooms are
attractive, with great coastal
views; the pool is large and
deep. Pet-lovers will
appreciate the company of
several dogs and cats, and
only the sound of extensive

bird life can impede on the serenity of it all ❷.

Sundale Guesthouse

Map 3, F4. Sunny Acres ⊤ 452-4120.

Paul Kingshott's small, tightly run guesthouse on a side road near the Gablewoods Mall is scrupulously clean, inexpensive and within walking distance of Choc Bay's beaches. Rooms have verandahs, fans and private bath with hot water, and the three one-bedroom apartments can sleep four at a push. There's a communal lounge with TV and VCR, and breakfast is included in the rates. No credit cards. ❷

Windjammer Landing

Map 3, F2. Labrellotte Bay ⊤ 456-9000, 1-800/267-7600 (Canada), 0/800-316-9797 (UK), 1-800/743-9609 (US), ⓕ 452-9454, ⓦ www.windjammer -landing.com.

Sprawled over 55 hillside acres on and above Labrellotte Bay, with accommodation ranging from luxury rooms to self-contained villas, some containing up to four bedrooms, some with private pools, all with stunning views. Golf carts shuttle you around between the site's four restaurants (one is beachside), four pools and the beach, which offers watersports. The unequalled kid-friendly atmosphere makes this a top choice for families. Rooms ❻, cottages ❼

Wyndham Morgan Bay Resort

Map 3, F2. Choc Bay ⊤ 450-2511 or 1-800/996-3426 (US), ⓕ 450-1050; in US ⊤ 1-800/996-3426, ⓦ www.wyndham.com.

This all-inclusive monolith is well equipped, welcoming and a good choice for families and travellers who like to know what to expect from their hotel chain. The somewhat gaudy rooms are large and the grounds and beach are pleasant and impeccably kept. Lots of Butlins-meets-Eurocamp-meets-YMCA-style activities keep guests busy and the two restaurants, beach café and bar serve more than adequate food and drink – and lots of it – all day long. Most watersports are included. ❼

CASTRIES AND AROUND

GROS ISLET AND THE NORTH

As St Lucia's tourist heartland, the island's northern tip is plentifully supplied with large resorts, medium-sized hotels and inexpensive guesthouses, the majority of which are located in the "Golden Mile" between **Rodney Bay** and **Gros Islet**. Despite the area's popularity, accommodation is no more expensive than in less busy parts of the country, and proximity to beaches, watersports, golf, shopping, restaurants and tour companies make it the ideal spot if you like to be in the thick of things. Being so near the capital, public transport is abundant, the coastal roads are good, and there's a lot of opportunity for exploring both the coast and interior (though for the latter, you'll need a rugged car, preferably with 4WD).

While the town of Gros Islet is a little grim outside of the Friday night jump-up, accommodation is cheap and just a stone's throw away from happening Rodney Bay.

RODNEY BAY

- - - - - - - - - - - - - - - - - - -

Bay Gardens Hotel

Map 4, F9. Castries–Gros Islet Highway ⓣ452-8060, ⓕ452-8059, ⓦwww.baygardenshotel .com.

Set in almost incandescent lemon-lime buildings gathered around a free-form pool and lushly landscaped gardens, the a/c rooms have verandahs, TVs, coffee-makers and minibars. Those on the second floor overlooking the pool have the best views. Reduit Beach is just down the road, accessible by a free shuttle. ❸

Candyo Inn

Map 4, E8. ⓣ452-0712 or 452-4599, ⓕ452-0774, ⓦwww.candyoinn.com.

Close to some of the island's best swimming spots and restaurants (it's 5min on foot to Reduit Beach) yet surprisingly quiet; you won't be bothered by crowds. Decorated with florals, pinks and potted plants, standard rooms and apartment suites are sizeable; the latter come with kitchenettes and separate sitting rooms. There's a small pool and snack bar. ❸

Ginger Lily

Map 4, E7. ☏ 458-0300, ⓕ 452-0012, ⓦ www.rodneybay.com. Intimate hotel with eleven colourful, well-equipped rooms and suites with a personal touch. Freshwater pool, internet access, cable TV and a/c, and all right by one of the finest beaches on the island. ❸

Harmony Marina Suites

Map 4, E8. ☏ 452-8756 or 452-0336, ⓕ 452-8677, ⓦ www.harmonysuites.com. One of the original hotels on Rodney Bay's marina, next door to Pepper's mini market around 200 yards from Reduit Beach, this place has a pool and tropical garden. The thirty bland but comfortable suites have fridges, coffee-makers, hair dryers, etc; 22 of them sleep up to four adults while the deluxe waterfront ones sleep two and have private sundecks and indoor jacuzzis. Twelve "apartment suites" have kitchens, but the marina-side restaurant, the *Mortar & Pestle*, is reasonable. Suite rates: ❸, ❹ with kitchen.

Kai Caribe

Map 4, E8. Reduit Beach ☏ 552-8898, ⓕ 452-0093. These three one-bedroom villas are beautifully designed and share a swimming pool despite being just a few minutes walk from Reduit Beach. One home – the Loft – is on two floors, separated by a handsome wooden stairway. For three people add $10–$15 per night. ❸

Rainbow Hotel

Map 4, E6. Reduit Beach ☏ 452-0148, ⓕ 452-0158, ⓦ www.rainbowstlucia.com. Hotel with 76 spacious and comfortable rooms, most of which overlook the pool. The atmosphere is cosy for a place so big and there's a restaurant, bar and fitness centre on site. Reduit Beach is right across the street. ❹

RODNEY BAY

Rex St Lucian

Map 4, E7. Reduit Beach
ⓣ 452-8351 or 1-800/255-5829
(US) or 02087/415 333 (Europe),
ⓕ 452-8331, ⓦ www.rexresorts
.com.

Having recently swallowed up
the baby of the *Rex Resorts*
family, the *Rex Papillon*, the
Rex St Lucian is now the
larger of the two sister resorts
on Reduit Beach and offers
sizeable if sterile rooms with
all amenities, restaurants,
cafés, tennis and watersports.
The big attractions are the
beach in front and the
plethora of Rodney Bay
restaurants. For up to three
adults or two adults plus two
kids; minimum stay three
nights. ❻

Royal St Lucian

Map 4, E7. Reduit Beach
ⓣ 452-9999, ⓕ 452-9639; in US
ⓣ 1-800/255-5859, in Europe
ⓣ 02087/415 333;
ⓦ www.rexresorts.com.
Right next to its sister
property on the popular
Reduit Beach, the *Royal St
Lucian* has 96 lavish suites and
three restaurants; the pool –
with bridges, a waterfall and

interconnecting waterways –
is an attraction in itself. In
addition to its location and all
the usual top deck amenities,
there's a spa on site. For up to
three adults or two adults plus
two kids, minimum stay three
nights: ❼

Tuxedo Villas

Map 4, E7. Reduit Beach 452-
8553, ⓕ 452-8577.
These ten bright villas across
the street from Reduit Beach
might be scant on atmosphere
but boast all mod cons. Two-
bedroom, two-bathroom
units represent good value for
larger groups, and there are
one-bedroom villas as well.
There's a restaurant, pool and
bar on site. One bedroom ❹,
two bedroom ❻.

Villa Zandoli

Map 4, E8, Reduit Beach
ⓣ 452-8898, ⓕ 452-0093,
ⓦ www.saintelucie.com
A really special, brightly
painted guesthouse with a
single, two twins and two
doubles; the owner also has
three one-bedroom
apartments across the way.
The guesthouse rooms are

cheery and large and there's a communal area, barbecue, free internet access and well-equipped kitchen. Bathrooms are shared. ❷

GROS ISLET AND AROUND

- - - - - - - - - - - - - - - - - - -

Alexander's Guesthouse

Map 4, E5. Marie Therese Street, Gros Islet ☎450-8610, ⓕ452-5428.

Ten inexpensive, spartan rooms near to the sometimes dirty Gros Islet beach. Two rooms have kitchenettes (others have use of the owner's kitchen to make breakfast), most rooms share the hot-water bathrooms and there's a communal TV lounge. The proximity of the Friday night street party inevitably means some weekend commotion. ❷

Bay Mini Guesthouse

Map 4, E5. Bay Street, Gros Islet ☎&ⓕ450-8956, ⓔbaymini@hotmail.com.

Right on Gros Islet's public beach, convenient for public transport and about a minute's walk from the loud Friday night jump-up, this small guesthouse has both adequate standard rooms and studios with kitchens; all feature private bathroom, fans and mosquito nets. No credit cards. ❷

Daphil's Hotel

Map 4, E6. Marie Therese Street, Gros Islet ☎450-9318, ⓕ452-4387, ⓦwww.geocities.com/daphilshotel

Pink, tall and cheap, this ten-room inn is close to the beach, just across the street from Gros Islet's public library. The smallish rooms have private baths, fans or a/c; those on the second floor have ocean or street views. Breakfast is available for US$5. ❷

Glencastle Resort

Map 4, G6. Massade ☎450-0833, ⓕ450-0837, ⓦwww.glencastleresort.net.

Just off the main highway, on a hill above Gros Islet with views of Rodney Bay and its marina, this small hotel has serviceable rooms with balconies, a/c and cable TV set in a two-storey building around the central pool and deck. It's a bit lifeless and tattered, but good value and convenient for excursions to west-coast beaches and the Gros Islet street party. ❸

La Panache Guesthouse

Map 4, G5. Cas-en-Bas Road Ⓣ450-0765, ⒻF450-0453, Ⓦwww.lapanache.com.
Scattered on a hill with views west to Gros Islet, the seven colourful rooms all have private baths, mosquito nets and fans. There's a photograph-festooned restaurant (see p.187) offering excellent twice-weekly feasts, a gazebo-style lounge with TV and books to borrow, and Cas-en-Bas beach is only around 1500m to the east. ❷

Nelson's Furnished Apartments

Map 4, G5. Cas-en-Bas Road ⓉF450-8275, ⒻF450-9108, Ⓔnelsonapartment@hotmail.com.
Mr Nelson's six apartments are not deluxe, but they have full kitchens, private baths, fans and cable TV. Hot water

is available, usually in the evenings. The location on the road to Cas-en-Bas is good for exploring the north end of the island and, if you've got a 4WD, the beaches on the east coast. ❷

Stephanie's Hotel

Map 4, G5. Castries–Gros Islet Highway, Massade ⓉF450-8689, ⒻF450-8134, Ⓦwww.geocities.com/bb_hotel.
Twenty rooms, some with kitchens, on the east side of the busy Castries–Gros Islet Highway, convenient for exploring Rodney Bay, but a bit noisy. Some rooms have a kitchenette, there's a small lobby with TV and an inexpensive local bar/restaurant/pizza joint below. ❷

CAP ESTATE AREA

Hotel CAPri

Map 4, G1. Smugglers Cove, Cap Estate ⓉF450-0009, ⒻF450-0002, Ⓦwww.capristlucia.com.
This adorable ten-room guesthouse nestled in the hills above Smuggler's Cove is the

perfect getaway for independent travellers and those who like a touch of home and camaraderie. The well-appointed rooms all have stunning views of the bay, there's an open-air honesty bar, a reasonable restaurant and rates include breakfast. All guests have free access to the Oasis spa facilities at neighbouring *LeSPORT* (see below) and there are yoga, tai-chi and meditation classes on an outdoor wooden deck overlooking the pool and herb garden below. Gay-friendly. ❹

LeSPORT – The Body Holiday

Map 4, G1. Cap Estate ⓣ450-8551 or 1-800/544-2883 (US),

ⓕ450-0368;

ⓦ www.thebodyholiday.com. One of the island's few all-inclusive resorts that manages to escape the Butlins/*Dirty Dancing* associations and make singles feel comfortable. On the downside, rooms are somewhat barren and cold and the beach is just adequate, but the emphasis is on getting you out, about and active – for a price. It's usually full of stressed-out city types indulging in the all-inclusive spa treatments, exercise classes, hikes, watersports, golf lessons, archery and tai-chi. The food is plentiful, healthful and well-prepared, especially at the *Tao* restaurant. ❼

SOUFRIÈRE AND THE WEST COAST

Staying along the west coast **between Castries and Soufrière** is ideal if you want to get away from heavily traf-ficked tourist areas and relax in some of the finest resorts and guesthouses on the island. The beaches are inviting and uncrowded, and the limited number of accommodation choices (the vast majority in **Marigot Bay** or **Soufrière**) tend to be less resort-like than those further north. Staying in peaceful Marigot isn't a cheap option, but there are sev-eral budget hotels and guesthouses in downtown Soufrière, as well as luxurious resorts on its outskirts. Public transport north and south of Soufrière is frequent; see p.116 for details.

MARIGOT BAY

Inn on the Bay

Map 1, D6. ⓣ 451-4260, ⓦ www.saint-lucia.com.
Set 90m up on a hillside at the south side of the bay, this pleasant five-room guesthouse exudes peace, quiet and relaxation. Spacious rooms with fridges surround the deck and pool, the hosts are extremely knowledgeable about the island, and the sea breeze wafting up the hill renders a/c unnecessary while also discouraging the mosquitoes. Continental breakfast is included. ❹

Marigot Beach Club

Map 1, D6. ⓣ 451-4974, ⓕ 451-4973.
Ensconced on the north side of the bay and a couple of minutes from the road's end by water taxi, the location has long been the main draw at this hotel; the open-air restaurant is named *Doolittle's*

(see p.189) after the Rex Harrison movie filmed here in the 1960s. Villas and studios – brimming with amenities – come with kitchen/kitchenettes, and the pool, beach, watersports and shops will keep you busy. Studios ❸, villas ❺

Oasis Marigot

Map 1, D6. ⓣ 1-800/263-4202 (US & Canada), 0-800/2765-8241 (UK & worldwide), ⓕ 1-305/946-6372, ⓦ www.oasismarigot.com.
A vast selection of villas, apartments and cottages nestled in the hills on both shores of the bay, *Oasis Marigot* offers a great blend of cosy and exotic with fully furnished kitchens, balconies, alfresco dining areas and private dipping pools. Cottages ❹, villas ❺

Sea Horse Inn

Map 1, D6. ⓣ 451-4436, ⓕ 451-4872, ⓦ www.seahorse-inn.com.
Reached via water taxi from

the docks, this elegant but simple getaway on the north side of the bay is set in a 1920s stone house and run by a kindly, protective Canadian couple and their two lovely dogs. The five rooms have mosquito nets, overhead fans and en-suite bathrooms, there's a small pool and a pleasant public room with bar overlooking the bay. Rates include breakfast and ferry passes. Generally there's a seven-night minimum stay. ❹

Ti Kaye Village

Map 1, C7. ☎456-8101, ℻456-8105, ⓦwww.tikaye.com. Spacious wooden cottages, large four-poster beds, private outdoor showers and verandahs with hammocks, all in a remote west coast setting overlooking Anse Cochon, make this one of the island's most secluded and romantic spots to stay. The beach is accessed via a steep set of wooden stairs leading down from the handsome restaurant. Scuba diving is available and an excellent full breakfast is included in the rates. ❻

SOUFRIÈRE AND AROUND

Anse Chastanet

Map 5, A1. Anse Chastanet ☎459-7000 or 1-800/223-1108 (US), ℻459-7700, ⓦwww.ansechastanet.com. Genteel, old-style resort spread over a hill above Soufrière's nicest beach. The larger rooms are extortionately priced, but are spacious and airy and reminiscent of luxurious treehouses (some have branches growing through the floors), with lovely ocean or mountain views and open porches; basic rooms are still incredibly pricey but much less unique. The reception and one restaurant are on an upper level, the beach and another eatery are 100 steps below. There's a great in-house diving and jungle biking outfit (see p.24), and the snorkelling here is very good. ❼

Chez Camille

Map 5, C4. Church St and Boulevard St, Soufrière ⓣ459-5379, ⓕ459-5684. *Camilla's* restaurant on Bridge Street (see p.190) is the contact for these two downtown guesthouses, both called *Chez Camille* and separated by a couple of blocks. Rooms are cosy, bright and secure with fans and mosquito nets; most share cold-water bathrooms. Each location has a small common room with a TV. Guests get a ten percent discount in *Camilla's* restaurant. No credit cards. ❸

Fond Doux Estate Guesthouse

Map 5, G6. Castries–Soufrière Road ⓣ 459-7545, ⓕ459-7882. Two charming and elegant rooms in a period cottage on a working cocoa plantation (see p.111), with beautiful gardens harbouring a wide array of flowers and fruit trees. Guests may use the plantation-house kitchen and pick fruit from the grounds; the on-site restaurant is excellent. Rates include breakfast. ❷

Hummingbird Beach Resort

Map 5, A1. Anse Chastanet Road ⓣ459-7232 or 459-7492, ⓕ459-7033, ⓦwww.nvo.com/pitonresort/home. Pleasant, moderately priced inn on the north side of the beach with a decent restaurant (see p.191). Furnished with reproduction plantation antiques (some have four-poster beds), the nine rooms and cottage have overhead fans, mosquito nets and louvred windows, not all are en-suite and only some have a private balcony. The beach in front leaves a lot to be desired, but Anse Chastenet is a thirty-minute walk away, and there is a pool. A country cottage across the road sleeps four. Rooms ❸, cottage ❺

Jalousie Hilton Resort and Spa

Map 5, E7. Anse des Pitons. Reservations ⓣ456-8042 or 1-888/744-5256 (US); hotel ⓣ456-8000, ⓕ456-8042, www.jalousie-hilton.com. Despite both an absolutely stunning setting between the Pitons, and efforts to make the chain's St Lucian venture feel like anything but a *Hilton*, this resort lacks the individuality and romantic charm of others in its price category. The mountain views and luxury amenities – private plunge pools, spa and fitness facilities, individual cottages and imported white sand from Guyana – should make this paradise, but the effect is rather more of a soulless playground for the rich. Food is costly but good, if often far from local, and as no private cars are allowed to drive the hundreds of *Hilton* acres, guests must walk or rely on hotel shuttles and may find themselves compelled to stay on site. ➐

Ladera Resort

Map 5, F7. Soufrière–Vieux Fort Road ☏459-7323 or 1-800/841-4145 (US), ⨍459-5156. Views are key in this unusual hillside resort, which looks down 300m over the Pitons and the bay. Deliberately open to the elements, rooms are without a back wall in order to maximize both the vista and the sense of being at one with nature; night-time tree-frog concertos, mosquitoes and the sulphurous smell from the springs below add to the sensation. Most rooms have plunge pools where the "fourth wall" should be and the restaurant, *Dasheen* (see p.190), has an excellent reputation, although you should expect at least this much quality and quirkiness for the price. ➐

La Haut Plantation Resort

Map 5, C1. Castries–Soufrière Road ☏459-7008, ⨍454-5975, www.lahaut.com. Set on a working plantation a couple of kilometres north of town, these five rooms are spacious and comfortable, with kitchenettes, ceiling fans, and wonderful views of the hills and Pitons. The restaurant (see p.191) is reasonably priced and serves delicious local food while the poolside bar is perfect for a

SOUFRIÈRE AND AROUND

sunset drink. An excellent continental breakfast is included. ❸

La Mirage Guesthouse

Map 5, C4. 14 Church St, Soufrière, ☏459-7010. Owner John Lamontagne worked as a chef in London for nearly forty years before returning home and opening *La Mirage* guesthouse and restaurant (see p.192) in 1998. The four rooms are clean and basic, but comfortable and good value with en-suite bathrooms, a mini-fridge and a balcony overlooking Church Street. No credit cards. ❷

Mago Estate Hotel

Map 5, B1. Soufrière–Castries Road ☏459-7352 or 459-5880, ⓦwww.magohotel.com. Six (soon to be twelve) rather special rooms, with four-poster beds, private stone terraces and heavy wooden shutters opening out to the garden and town below. Yoga, tai-chi and massages are on offer and there's a fresh water pool boasting a bar housed in the roots of a mango tree.

The restaurant – serving somewhat overpriced, standard local cuisine – is of a similar design. Rates include continental breakfast. ❸

Still Plantation Resort

Map 5, G3. Fond St Jacques Road ☏459-5179 or 459-7261, ⓕ459-7301, ⓦwww.thestillresort .com. Out on the road to Fond St Jacques, near the turnoff for the Diamond Waterfall, this peaceful escapist's guesthouse is set on a 400-acre working cocoa plantation. The modern studios and apartments are incredibly spacious and quiet, the latter have kitchens, all have fans and some a/c. There's a restaurant, large pool and bar on site, and the beach/town shuttles are complimentary. The owner offers plantation tours on horseback. ❷, ❸ with kitchen and a/c.

Still Beach Resort

Map 5, A1. Anse Chastanet Road ☏459-5179 or 459-7261, ⓕ459-7301, ⓦwww.thestillresort .com.

This small inn on the north side of town has bright upstairs rooms cooled by overhead fans and the sea breeze; some have kitchens and TV, all have mosquito nets and are linked by a common balcony above the deservedly popular waterfront restaurant and bar (see p.193). The beach here is sufficient, but it's not the island's best. ❸, ❹ with kitchen.

Stonefield Estate

Map 5, C7. Soufrière–Vieux Fort Road Ⓣ459-5648 or 459-7037, Ⓕ459-5550, Ⓦwww.stonefieldvillas.com These ten spacious villas occupying the well-manicured grounds of an old plantation may be Soufrière's best kept secret; designed and decorated with nature in mind, they rival the aesthetic of any of the area's luxury hotels at a fraction of the cost. Each airy villa has separate kitchen and sleeping areas, hammocked wooden balconies affording glorious views of the Pitons, slatted wooden windows and wonderfully spacious and private open-air showers, with flowers trailing all around. A pool, restaurant (*Mango Tree*, see p.192) and bar are situated to maximize the mountain views and beach shuttles are free. ❻

THE SOUTH COAST

The area **south of Soufrière**, through the fishing villages of Choiseul and Laborie, is more residential than tourist-oriented and offers a relaxed alternative to the relentless activity of the northwest coast. Several excellent guest-houses can be found on or near the inviting beaches that line the coastal road from Soufrière to Vieux Fort. **Vieux Fort** itself also hosts several decent hotels and guesthouses, within easy reach of the international airport.

Balenbouche Estate

Map 1, C13. Balenbouche Bay ⓣ455-1244, ⓕ455-1342, ⓦwww.balenbouche.com.
Scattered with fruit trees, remains of old plantation buildings and even a few Amerindian rock carvings, this charming and slightly dilapidated 80-acre plantation just south of Choiseul is most welcoming. The rooms – some in the estate house and others in adjacent cottages – are clean and cosy; some share baths, some have cold water only and cottages have kitchens Anse Touloulou beach is a brief walk away. Rates include breakfast. ❷, cottages ❹

Kimatrai Hotel

Map 1, F14. Vieux Fort ⓣ454-6328, ⓕ454-3038, ⓦwww.kimatraihotel.com
Bright and airy new rooms with tiled bathrooms, cable TV, mini-fridges and a/c; studios and apartments come with kitchens and overlook Vieux Fort's fishing port and the Caribbean. An onsite restaurant and bar make this a good choice if you arrive late at night. Rooms (including continental breakfast) ❷, apartments ❷–❸.

Juliette's Lodge

Map 1, F14. Beanfield, Vieux Fort ⓣ454-5300, ⓕ454-5305, ⓦwww.julietteslodge.com.
The 27 a/c rooms here are comfortable and clean, the three apartments spacious and there's a lively restaurant (see p.194) serving basic but hearty fare. There's also a pool and mountain bikes available for hire; the beach is a few hundred yards down the road. ❸

Mirage Beach Resort

Map 1, D13. Laborie Bay, Laborie ⓣ455-9763, ⓕ455-9237, ⓦwww.cavip.com/mirage.
Right on the bay in the calm, beautiful fishing village of Laborie, this divine spot offers five well-appointed rooms by the water, some with kitchenette and terrace; the friendly owners also operate a French/Creole open-air restaurant and bar on site. ❷

Skyway Inn

Map 1, F14. Beanfield, Vieux Fort ☏ 454-7111, ⨍ 454-7116, ⓦ www.slucia.com/skyway. Your basic airport hotel, with large, comfortable rooms and a few studios, a pool, a bar popular with locals and a restaurant that's good for breakfast. The beach – with good windsurfing – is a couple of minutes away. ❸

THE EAST

There are only a couple of hotels between Vieux Fort and **Dennery**. This is a rural and primarily residential area characterized by fishing communities and striking, often deserted bays. However, there are a couple of nice spots to stay that make convenient bases if you're planning on exploring the central rainforests. North of Dennery, the coast is difficult to access, and accommodation choices are virtually non-existent.

Fox Grove Inn

Map 1, G9. Mon Repose ☏ 455-3800, ⨍ 455-3271, ⓦ www.foxgroveinn.com. Basic but charming and comfortable rooms located high in the hills several kilometres south of Dennery, within walking distance of Mamiku Gardens and with views of the popular Praslin Bay and Fregate Islands. The restaurant (see p.195) is renowned in St Lucia, serving excellent local cuisine, and the Swiss/St Lucian owners are knowledgeable and friendly. There's a swimming pool and pool table, but if you're looking for late night action, be aware that things here close around 10pm. Rates include breakfast. ❷

Manje Domi

Map 1, F11. Desruisseaux ☏ 455-0729, ⓦ www.slucia.com /manje/. Small guesthouse in the interior, about 13km from Vieux Fort; take the east-coast road toward Dennery, turn inland at the sign for Desruisseaux and proceed for about 2km. The Creole name means "Eat, Sleep," which pretty well sums it up. The restaurant (see p.195) is excellent, cosy and popular with locals, and it's a fine location to get away from crowds and explore the Des Cartiers Rainforest trails. Rooms are en suite with TV, there's a common room and a handsome verandah. Continental breakfast is included. ❷

Eating and drinking

Though St Lucia's restaurant scene is dominated by small, reasonably priced eateries with few pretensions, there are a few upmarket restaurants offering haute cuisine, and you're unlikely to be disappointed by them. The Castries Central Market stalls are excellent value, as are many of the local restaurants in Soufrière; the majority of St Lucia's restaurants, though, are clustered around the tourist areas. For a truly local experience, don't miss one of

RESTAURANT PRICES AND PAYMENT

The restaurants reviewed in this chapter have been graded inexpensive (US$10 or less), moderate (US$11–20), expensive (US$21–30) and very expensive (over US$30), based on the average price of a main meal excluding drinks and service charge.

Most restaurants in the tourist areas will accept credit cards, but small mom-and-pop operations like the barbecue pits at the Gros Islet street party probably won't. Restaurants generally tack on a ten percent service charge to your bill, meant to be a tip. Feel free to add extra if you feel the service warrants it – remember, the unfortunate truth is that some restaurants do not pass on the service charge to their staff.

the island's weekend fish fries – Anse La Raye on Friday nights and Dennery on Saturdays are the most rewarding.

A fair range of **cooking styles** splash the island's culinary map, but by far the most prevalent – and the best – is known, like the St Lucian language, as Creole. Heavily reliant on fresh seafood, fruits and exotic vegetables, Creole dishes reflect the history of the island's diverse population,

ST LUCIAN FOOD GLOSSARY

accra deep-fried salted cod fritter

boudin spicy blood sausage

breadfruit called *bwape* in Creole, these starchy, bland fruits grow on trees and are eaten fried or boiled

brochette skewered and barbecued meats and vegetables

callaloo leafy green vegetable that looks and tastes like spinach and is often used to make soup

carambola a sweet, star-shaped fruit

chataigne breadfruit-like fruit with large seeds, prepared as a vegetable side dish

christophene vegetable with white, watery flesh, eaten boiled or sautéed

colombo meat, usually goat, lamb or chicken, in a spicy curry sauce

dolphin a local, omnipresent and very tasty fish also known as dorado.

dasheen starchy root vegetable

fig green or ripe bananas

float deep-fried semi-sweet dough, sort of a St Lucian doughnut, so-named because it floats when fried; it's eaten as a snack on its own or as a side dish with fish

jerk method of seasoning meat, usually chicken, pork, or fish, with a multispice mixture heavy on pepper and pimento, which is then roasted slowly over wood or charcoal

mixing the spicy, tomato-based sauces and starchy carbo-hydrates of African-derived cooking with a flair for inventive garnishes, a throwback from years of French dominance (common Creole dishes and ingredients are listed in the glossary in the box below). Other options include Asian, French, Mexican, English and American Nouveau styles, while fast food exists in the form of basic burgers and

koko coconut in Creole

lambi conch

love apple tropical fruit with pulpy, sweet flesh

mago mango in Creole

papaya, pawpaw, papay in Creole; large orange or yellow fruit high in both vitamins and an enzyme used as a meat tenderizer

pepperpot soup spicy soup of beef and callaloo

plantain a larger, blander member of the banana family that turns from savoury to sweet as it ripens, and is eaten fried or boiled at either stage

roti flat, baked unleavened bread wrapped around a mix of curried vegetables or meat

saltfish salted cod

saltfish and green fig St Lucia's national dish of reconstituted, fried saltfish with cooked green banana

soursop a large, green, rough-skinned fruit that yields white, pulpy and sweet, not sour, flesh

sweetsop smaller version of a soursop

tamarind tropical tree that bears the pod from which acidic, sour fruit is eaten, also used to make relish-like syrups, candy and drinks

titiri small fish, deep-fried and eaten whole

ugli descriptive name of a hybrid citrus fruit, a cross between a grapefruit and tangerine, developed in Jamaica in the early 1900s

EATING AND DRINKING

barbecue, local pizza joints such as *Pizza! Pizza!*, *Key Largo* and *Peppino's* and a few imported *KFC* and *Dominos*.

Of available alcoholic **drinks**, the favourite local tipple is the very palatable Piton **beer**, brewed in Vieux Fort and dubbed the "Mystic Mountain Brew"; there's even a low-calorie version. A variation called Piton shandy borrows from the British tradition by mixing beer with something sweet, in this case ginger ale. St Lucia has also followed Caribbean tradition by producing some fine **rums**. St Lucia Distillers produces several brands; among the best are Old Fort Reserve, a smooth dark variety, and Denros, a strong white rum. Also on the shelves are Bounty (the island's best seller for its even taste), Five Blondes and Crystal brands. Those with a sweet tooth will appreciate several interesting rum **liqueurs**, among them La Belle Creole Black Satin coffee liqueur and Ti Tasse coffee rum liqueur, often mixed in exotic drinks or served after dinner with desserts and coffee. For a more down-to-earth local experience, the adventurous could try a **rum shop**, typically a wooden shack with rustic benches and bar stools, where you can buy simple groceries, a couple of basic beers, loose cigarettes and a lot of barely palatable white rum for around EC$1.50 at any time. You can pass the day watching the shop's more respectable customers come and go until nightfall, when the music starts to play. If rum isn't your spirit, you might find whisky, brandy or wine in more upscale establishments, but these are new takes on an old tradition. **Soft drinks** such as Pepsi are both imported and bottled locally, and distilled water is widely available, although the tap water is generally safe to drink. For a cheap and healthy alternative, try **coconut water**. Drunk straight from the opened husk of a green nut, the juice is naturally sterilized and rich in potassium and other minerals. You'll find vendors at the markets and roadside stands throughout the island.

EATING AND DRINKING

Like many of St Lucia's shops and businesses, some of the island's restaurants are closed on Sundays, except for those affiliated with hotels. Also note that during the off-season, **opening hours** and days might change, and some restaurants close for up to a month at a time. While we've given opening hours for most establishments, many will stay open as long as they have customers; it's best to call ahead for **reservations**, particularly in the high season – some restaurants will even transport you to and from your hotel at no extra cost.

CASTRIES

There are a few places to eat downtown, good for grabbing a quick bite while shopping or sightseeing – by far the best of these are the stalls at **Castries Central Market**. You'll probably be lunching with local businesspeople on their break, a situation that holds the downtown eateries to high standards and uninflated prices. For a more formal meal, head into the surrounding hills, where stunning views accentuate the experience.

Castries Central Market
Map 2, E4. Jeremie St ⊤ 453-6580. Daily 6am–5pm.
Inexpensive.
Market vendors, shoppers and local businesspeople flock to eat breakfast or lunch at these dozen or so restaurant stalls in a small, crowded alleyway behind the market. Taken at unadorned plastic tables, the servings of seafood, rotis, rice and beans or meat and dumplings are hearty and delicious. Most stalls don't accept credit cards.

Jammin' Juice
Map 2, D6. Corner of Manoel and Brazil streets. Inexpensive.
A fun new place on the main road south out of central Castries, *Jammin' Juice* is great for freshly made smoothies,

CASTRIES

juices, and healthy snacks. Opening hours were not set at time of writing.

The Monkey Tree Café
Map 2, E4. Corner of Cadet and Jeremie streets ⊤451-3004.
Mon–Fri 7am–5pm, Sat 7am–3pm, Sun cruise ship days only. **Inexpensive.**
Feels like a mini-canteen but serves better food: local dishes, salads and the "hot plate cooking" system, where you can choose a little from a variety of main and side dishes to create your own meal. Cheap and filling, at least.

Peppino's Pizza
Map 2, D7. Upper Bridge St ⊤457-7466. Daily: lunch & dinner. **Inexpensive.**
Good pizza, calzones, and some traditional Italian pasta dishes are the fare at this typical pizza joint. There's another branch at the Gablewoods Mall north of town.

AROUND CASTRIES

Several very good restaurants – and a couple that rank amongst St Lucia's very best – are found around the Vigie Peninsula, Morne Fortune and the hills to the east of Castries. Catering to an upscale business community, they are renowned for innovative cuisine and a more sophisticated urban ambience than you'll encounter elsewhere on the island. Popular with both tourists and local people, most are usually busy, so reservations are recommended. North of Castries, along the Castries–Gros Islet Highway, is the Choc Bay area, with several beachside restaurants and bars that are worth a visit for their relaxed, oceanside atmosphere and solid fare.

MORNE FORTUNE

Bon Appetit

Map 3, B8. Morne Road, Morne Fortune ☎ 452-2757.
Mon–Fri 11am–2pm & 6.30–9.30pm, Sat & Sun 6.30–9.30pm. **Expensive.**
Reservations are essential at this popular, rather expensive five-table restaurant in a guesthouse (see p.156) in the Castries hills. House specialties are steaks and seafood; the cuisine is international and French Nouveau – smallish servings tastefully arranged and embellished with minimal amounts of heavy sauces – and the wine selection is as impressive as the views of the harbour below.

Green Parrot Inn

Map 3, B8. Morne Fortune ☎ 452-3399 or 452-3167.
Daily 7am–late. Expensive.
Irascible chef Harry Edwards trained at the illustrious *Claridge's* hotel in London, but now he's content with presiding over Wednesday and Saturday night floorshows and cooking up Creole, West Indian and international food with flair. The seafood here is great and there are views down onto Castries Harbour. Ladies wearing flowers in their hair, accompanied by well-dressed gents, eat for free on Mondays; otherwise the prix-fixe (call for days) is EC$90. The restaurant will pay round-trip taxi fares for groups of four or more, or the one-way fare for parties of two.

VIGIE AND AROUND

Beach Facilities

Map 3, D5. Vigie Beach ☎ 452-5494.
Mon–Sat 10am–2pm.
Inexpensive.
Small, dark and right on the beach at the east end of the airport runway, offering hearty local food with no frills – mutton stew, fried fish, curried chicken etc. Things liven up at night with occasional live or canned

AROUND CASTRIES

181

music and entertainment. No credit cards.

The Coal Pot

Map 3, B5. Vigie Marina, Vigie ☎452-5566. Mon–Fri lunch & dinner, Sat dinner only. Expensive to very expensive.

One of the island's busiest restaurants and probably the best – dinner reservations are essential. The New World cuisine is French-influenced, decorative and pricey, but the seafood is fresh and the salads are recommended. Directly on the water's edge, the dark interior is embellished with local artwork; this is a perfect place for a special night out.

D's Restaurant

Map 3, E4. Edgewater Beach Club, Vigie Beach ☎453-7931. Mon–Sat 11am–11pm. Moderate.

Beachside bistro with a touch of elegance, specializing in Creole seafood dishes. The waterside setting is appealing, and the food won't disappoint either.

Froggie Jack's

Map 3, C6. Vigie Marina ☎458-1900. Mon–Sat lunch & dinner. Moderate.

A warm, personal bar and restaurant that's big on excellent food and small on overdressed pomp. The restaurant sits above the marina and the fare is prepared to order by an experienced French chef with an emphasis on seafood and home-smoked meats.

The Wharf Restaurant and Bar

Map 3, F3. Castries–Gros Islet Highway, Choc Bay ☎450-4844. Daily 9am–midnight. Moderate.

Roadside/beachside joint serving standard bar fare and plenty of fish dishes, both local and American/European. The attraction is not the food but the access to their watersports facilities, showers and the beach. Weekend BBQs with live music, competitions and dancing on the beach.

GROS ISLET AND THE NORTH

Back-to-back restaurants in the busy "Golden Mile" north of Castries provide a staggering number of choices. Beachside eateries along Reduit Beach offer dining with sea breezes, and Rodney Bay as a whole seems to have more restaurants per square mile than anywhere else on the island, most clustered around the intersection of the Castries–Gros Islet highway and Reduit Beach Road. During the Friday night street party in Gros Islet, restaurateurs and vendors set up roadside barbecues and sell roasted chicken, fish or meats, as well as cold beers to wash it down. North of Gros Islet, the restaurants thin out a bit, but a number of vendors set up in front of the entrance to Pigeon Point and at the causeway beach, selling tasty barbecued chicken, roasted vegetables and floats. East of Gros Islet, on the road to Cas-en-Bas, *La Panache* is a fun experience and boasts one of the area's more authentic Creole menus.

RODNEY BAY

Big Chef Steakhouse

Map 4, G8. Rodney Bay Marina ☏ 450-0210.
Mon–Sat from 6pm. **Moderate.**
Popular local-TV chef caters for those who like their meal full-on carnivorous. From an 8oz tenderloin to "as big as you can handle", these steaks are not for the faint hearted – or the gourmet. Pasta and seafood is available, if you must.

Capone's

Map 4, E8. ☏ 452-0284.
Tues–Sun lunch & dinner.
Moderate to expensive.
One of the string of restaurants in Rodney Bay's eating epicentre, serving somewhat overrated and uninspired Italian dinners in a gangster-inspired ambience – drinks include a good-sized Mafia Mai Tai. The small *Pizza Park* pizzeria next door is open from 11am to midnight.

The Cat's Whiskers

Map 4, E7. ℡452-8880.
Tues–Sun 8am–late. **Moderate.**
Unassuming restaurant serving hearty traditional English fare from full breakfasts to ploughman's lunches and steak and kidney pies with hand-cut chips, as well as reasonable brews on tap (EC$8). The popular Sunday brunch is a feast: roast beef, Yorkshire pudding and all the trimmings.

Charthouse

Map 4, E8. Rodney Bay Marina ℡452-8115.
Mon–Sat 5–11pm. **Expensive.**
Steaks, ribs and lobster are the specialities, and as they're cooked better here than anywhere else on the island, reservations are essential. Vegetarians take note: there's little to nothing of interest for you on the menu here. The dark-wood, marina-side restaurant (reserve seats on the waterside deck) also serves other seafood and Creole dishes. Top it off with a Cuban cigar, on sale at the restaurant.

Eagles Inn

Map 4, F6. Reduit Beach Road ℡452-0650.
Daily: lunch & dinner. **Moderate.**
A good lunch spot at the far end of the Reduit Beach Road, up against the Rodney Bay marina channel, specializing in grilled and barbecued seafood, chicken and ribs. The waterside setting is pleasant, and you're just across the street from the beach.

Elena's Italian Ice Cream

Map 4, E8. ℡458-0576.
Daily 10am–11 pm.
Inexpensive.
The owner's father owned a top notch *gelateria* in Italy, and here the tradition and artisanship involved in true Italian ice-cream making has been brought to St Lucia, with a mouthwatering collection of eighteen delectable, home-made flavours served right by the beach.

Key Largo

Map 4, G8. Castries–Gros Islet Highway ℡452-0282.

Daily 9am–11pm. **Moderate.**
Casual pizza place on the east side of the Castries–Gros Islet Highway, across from the marina, serving by far the best pizza on the island, fired up in a wood-fueled brick oven. Excellent pasta dishes and freshly squeezed juices also available.

La Creole
Map 4, G8. Rodney Bay Marina ☎ 450-0022.
Daily 11.30am–10pm. **Moderate to expensive.**
Commanding an excellent position on the marina and specializing, unsurprisingly, in Creole dishes with the emphasis on seafood. You can even pick your lobster from the restaurant aquarium if you've got the nerve. For dessert, try the home-made peanut ice cream. There's dancing every evening and occasional live music.

The Lime
Map 4, E8. ☎ 452-0761.
Daily, breakfast, lunch & dinner. **Moderate.**
"Liming" is West Indian slang for "hanging out", and this is

one of Rodney Bay's more popular spots to do just that. The eclectic menu is a mix of palatable steaks and seafood done in spicy tomato sauces "Lucian style", with indoor and alfresco (on the patio next to the road) dining, and live music weekly – Sunday is karaoke night.

Memories of Hong Kong
Map 4, E9. ☎ 452-8218.
Mon–Sat 4.30pm–late.
Moderate.
Traditional and very good Cantonese and Asian delicacies are the main fare here at the island's only open-kitchen (read noisy) restaurant.

Miss Saigon
Map 4, E8. ☎ 452-0580.
Daily 5pm–midnight. **Moderate.**
Owner Myrna Esquillo hails from the Philippines and her fine, if small, eatery on a side street near the main Rodney Bay drag serves delicate and tasty Southeast Asian cuisine; try the king prawns in Thai green curry sauce, or the creamy lamb korma. The Asian dishes are vastly

GROS ISLET AND THE NORTH

preferable to the standard grilled ribs, fish and steaks also on offer. Seating is inside or alfresco.

Pizza! Pizza!
Map 4, E8. ℡452-8282.
Mon, Tues, Thurs & Sun 11am–midnight, Wed, Fri & Sat 11am–2am. **Inexpensive.**
The owners have sunk some money – but not a lot – into this hallway-sized pizza joint-cum-takeaway. It's in the same building as *Elena's Italian Ice Cream* and the only seating is outside in a small garden and playground by the marina.

Razmataz
Map 4, E7. Reduit Beach Road ℡452-9800. 4pm–late, closed Thurs. **Moderate.**
If you're a fan of Indian food, then this popular Reduit Beach restaurant is your best bet. Specialities are spicy vindaloo, korma and tikka masala, all prepared with tandoori (grilled) chicken, lamb or beef – there are plenty of non-meat options as well, plus occasional live music.

Roof Garden
Map 4, E8. ℡458-0565.
5pm–2am, closed Tues. **Very expensive.**
This pleasant if somewhat overpriced restaurant offers BBQ steaks, lobster, seafood, pasta and chicken served with local fruits and vegetables. There's live jazz with a late night menu from 11pm to 2am and a happy hour from 5 to 7pm. Both the indoor and outdoor seating are lovely.

Spinnakers
Map 4, E7. Reduit Beach ℡452-8491.
Daily 9am–11pm. **Moderate.**
Appealing lunch and dinner spot serving an international mix of steaks, grilled seafood, salads and roti that's more upscale than you'd expect for a beach bar. The setting is hard to beat, especially at sunset.

Thai Royal
Map 4, E8. ℡452-9249.
Daily 5–10.30pm. **Moderate to Expensive.**
Cooking that's more Thai–Chinese fusion than straight-up Thai. Rumour has it that the chefs once slaved in the

kitchens of the Sultan of Brunei and the food is certainly fit for royalty; try the satay appetizers and the banana mudslide desert.

Triangle Pub

Map 4, E8. ⊤452-0334. Daily 8am–late. **Inexpensive.**
The streetside *Triangle* is a cheap 'n' cheerful beach grill, and will happily barbecue everything but your socks. But they do it well, with all the trimmings, and also provide music. No credit cards, but with an average cost of EC$12, you probably won't be needing one.

GROS ISLET AND AROUND
- - - - - - - - - - - - - - - - - - -

La Panache

Map 4, G5. Cas-en-Bas Road ⊤450-0765.
No set hours. **Moderate.**
Twice a week, Henry Augustin lays on one of the area's best dining experiences at his friendly guesthouse (see also p.164); an informal, five-course feast of West Indian food at its finest. The menu is built around fresh fish, poultry and seasonally available market veggies, and dishes are passed around family-style, elbows and all. Call ahead to reserve a place.

CAP ESTATE AND AROUND
- - - - - - - - - - - - - - - - - - -

Captain's Cellar

Map 4, C2. Pigeon Island ⊤450-0918. Food served Mon–Fri 9am–9.30pm, Sat 9am–5pm, Sun 10am–9.30pm. **Inexpensive.**
A lovely, cavernous, traditional "English" pub housed in a 250-year-old building by the interpretation centre on Pigeon Island. It's free to get onto the "island" after 5pm, and here you'll find a wide selection of pub grub, from scrambled eggs and bacon to baked potatoes, salads and main dishes like chilli and risotto. Cheese and biscuits are available, as are BBQs on Saturday nights (7–9pm) and you can try your hand at darts or skittles.

GROS ISLET AND THE NORTH

Great House

Map 4, F1. Castries–Gros Islet Highway, Cap Estate ⊤450-0450. Tues–Sun 4.30–10pm. Expensive.

Fine dining (afternoon tea and dinner only) in a 235-year-old stone plantation house overlooking Becune Bay, with seating inside or on the stone patio. The cuisine is West Indian and French – try the lamb with garlic and rosemary – and the four-course set menu (around US$40) offers excellent value. Adjacent is the Derek Walcott amphitheatre, where you can see occasional works by the man himself before or after dinner, depending upon schedules.

Jambe de Bois/Snooty Agouti

Map 4, A3. Pigeon Island ⊤450-8166. Daily 9am–5pm. Inexpensive.

The legendary one-legged pirate François Leclerc – *jambe de bois* means "wooden leg" – who made Pigeon Point his home never ate in this café, but he didn't miss much. The food is uninspired, but it's a pleasant setting by the sea on Pigeon Island and a good place to cool off. Creole shrimp and chicken, fish and chips, burgers and sandwiches are all served.

SOUFRIÈRE AND THE WEST COAST

The coast road south of Castries hosts a small number of good-value eateries, and Soufrière holds its own against the tourism strongholds of the northwest, with a wealth of eating places ranging from small cafés to more elegant restaurants for relaxed evening dining. Some of the hotels also offer wide-ranging evening menus and comfortable beachside restaurants for lunching during the day.

MARIGOT BAY

Chateau Mygo
Map 1, D6. Marigot Bay Road
☏451-4772. Daily 7am–11pm.
Moderate.

Appealing, simple little restaurant at the end of the Marigot Bay road just before the water-taxi dock. Serving three meals per day, very much Creole style, with seating upstairs (inside and on the patio) and downstairs.

Doolittle's
Map 1, D6. ☏ 451-4974. Daily: lunch & dinner. Moderate to expensive.

Excellent sandwiches, salads and burgers at lunchtime and more elegant Caribbean fusion cuisine for both lunch and dinner are served in this lively spot right on the far side of the bay, set amidst palm trees and the perfect spot from which to view a Marigot sunset. BBQ on Saturday nights and live music Tues–Sun.

JJ's Paradise
Map 1, D6. Marigot Bay Road
☏451-4076. Daily 10am–late. Moderate.

The diminutive *JJ's* is on your left at the top of the hill just before Marigot Bay Road descends into Marigot Bay. The servings of simple Creole food are generous, and the restaurant occasionally hosts live bands.

The Shack
Map 1, D6. ☏ 451-4145
Lunch inexpensive, dinner moderate.

This casual floating timber café-restaurant lies over the water on stilts, and has an open-air veranda making it a great place to sit and take in the beach scene across the bay. Deliciously prepared sandwiches and salads at lunchtime, with a great Caribbean/American menu at dinner dominated by lots of super fresh seafood – the kingfish burgers, conch fritters and mahi mahi are highly recommended. Happy hour from 5pm to 7pm.

SOUFRIÈRE AND THE WEST COAST

SOUFRIÈRE AND AROUND

Bang

Map 5, E7. Anse des Pitons
ⓣ459-7864. Daily
noon–midnight. Moderate.
A fantastically located
restaurant, right on the water
at the south end of the
Jalousie Hilton resort (see
p.168) and between the
Pitons, reachable via water
taxi from town (around
EC$40 round trip, per
person). Serves spicy,
Jamaican jerk-style barbecued
fish, chicken and other meats.
There's a floorshow featuring
music, fire-eaters, limbo
dancers and acrobats on
Wednesdays

Camilla's

Map 5, B4. 7 Bridge St,
Soufrière ⓣ459-5379. Daily
8am–midnight. Inexpensive.
A clean, bright place just a
block from the waterfront,
with two tables on a small,
second-floor verandah
overlooking the street.
Vegetarian dishes such as
vegetable rotis are on offer, as

well as Creole-style fish,
lamb, pork and conch.
Breakfast is Creole fare like
saltfish and green fig, or eggs
with bacon.

Captain Hook's

Map 5, A1 Castries Rd
ⓣ758/459-7365. Inexpensive
to moderate.
This tiny local joint at the
southern end of Soufrière,
with plastic outdoor tables
and a less-than-inspired
interior, serves great prix-fixe
seafood dinners for EC$40
and huge portions of
delicious fish or chicken and
chips for EC$25.

Dasheene

Map 5, F7. Ladera Resort,
Soufrière-Vieux Fort Road
ⓣ459-7323. Daily 8–10am,
11am–2.30pm & 6.30pm–late.
Expensive.
Dasheene at the *Ladera Resort*
(see p.169) has a reputation as
the best restaurant in St
Lucia, although such
accolades may owe more to
the location than to the
uniform quality of the food.
The cuisine is an eclectic mix
of West Indian, Oriental,

Italian and vegetarian and is perhaps best explored at the EC\$50 Sunday Brunch or EC\$110 Monday buffet, both reasonably priced. The views of the Pitons and bay below are astonishing – come up for drinks before sunset and drift into dinner.

Fedo's

Map 5, C4. 10 Church St, Soufrière ☎459-5220. Mon–Fri 10am–7.30pm, Sat 10am–5pm. Inexpensive.

As there are only three tables, no decor to speak of and a menu limited to sandwiches, rotis, steak concoctions and seafood dishes, this is best for a quick but delicious snack. No credit cards.

Hummingbird Beach Resort

Map 5, A1. Anse Chastanet Road ☎459-7232. Daily: breakfast, lunch & dinner. Moderate.

Lush gardens surround this small and pricey hotel restaurant on the beach, which serves fresh juices, pastries, eggs and French toast for breakfast. Lunch and

dinner fare tends to be of the standard burgers, fish and fries variety. If you're dining, you can use the hotel's small pool, beach and showers (see also p.168).

Jalousie Hilton Resort

Map 5, E7. Anse des Pitons ☎459-7666. Daily: breakfast, lunch & dinner. Moderate to very expensive.

There are three pricey but tasty choices within this glitzy resort (see p.168); housed in the main Great House, the refined *Plantation* serves international cuisine (make reservations and dress up a bit), while on the water at the south end of the resort, the *Pier* is a more informal dinner option. On the beach, the *Bayside* serves lighter meals for breakfast and lunch, and lays on the occasional evening buffet with live entertainment.

La Haut Plantation Restaurant

Map 5, C1. *Le Haut Plantation Resort*, Castries-Soufrière Rd ☎459-7008. Tues–Sun, breakfast, lunch & dinner. Moderate.

SOUFRIÈRE AND THE WEST COAST

Very reasonably priced restaurant serving excellent, fresh local fare – and lots of it – in a gorgeous hillside setting overlooking the Pitons. The friendly staff will happily try to accommodate special requests.

La Mirage
Map 5, C4. *La Mirage Guesthouse*, 14 Church St ℡459-7010. Mon–Sat 11.30am–10pm. **Moderate.**
An informal ground-floor restaurant serving vegetarian specialities such as pasta and creative salads, as well as fish and chips, roasted chicken and pizza, all of which are substantial, sensibly priced and served with no fuss. Has a good reputation amongst locals.

Mango Tree Restaurant
Map 5, C7. *Stonefield Estate*, Soufriere–Vieux Fort Rd ℡459-7586. Daily 7.30am–10pm. **Moderate.**
One of St Lucia's newest and most enjoyable dining

experiences, in a rustic outdoor setting at the *Stonefield Estate* (see p.171). Delicious locally inspired menu featuring everything from fresh pumpkin soup to jerk chicken and vegetarian pasta dishes for lunch; freshly baked chocolate and banana cakes for afternoon tea (or breakfast); and seasonal vegetables with catch of the day fresh from the fish market in Soufrière for dinner.

Old Courthouse Restaurant
Map 5, C6. Soufrière waterfront ℡459-5002. Daily 8am–midnight. **Moderate to expensive**
This small but handsome waterfront building dates from 1898 – its bathrooms were once the courthouse cells. Cuisine is a popular fusion of West Indian and South East Asian styles and, despite a rather objectionable management attitude toward the help, reservations are essential in high season.

Pitons Restaurant

Map 5, A1. *Anse Chastanet*
☏459-7354. Daily: breakfast &
dinner. **Moderate to expensive.**
Overblown and somewhat
mediocre, if plentiful, fare:
the five-course menu
changes every day. The
setting, at the *Anse Chastanet*
resort (see p.167), is
impressive, looking across the
bay at Gros Piton. If you're
not driving, it's reachable via
water taxi from the Soufrière
waterfront (around EC$25
round trip).

Still Beach Resort

Map 5, A1. Anse Chastanet
Road ☏459-5179 or 459-7261.
Daily 7.30am–11pm. **Moderate.**
Served up under an ocean-
facing canopy on the beach,
with the waves lapping gently
all around, the three daily
meals here are mostly Creole-
based and spicy. Breakfast
ranges from saltfish and green
fig to omelette concoctions
and fresh coffee, while lunch
and dinner usually consist of
pepperpot soup, sweet-and-
sour flying fish or freshwater
prawns.

THE SOUTH COAST

Though there's less choice than along the north and west
coasts, the south has its share of good places to eat. There
are some reliable hotel restaurants near Hewanorra airport,
and for snacks, try the beach bars along the Anse de Sables
shoreline or the tasty fried fish sold along the section of
beach near to the *Chak Chak* restaurant. If you fancy some
Western-style fast food, there's a branch of *KFC* at JQ's
Plaza in Vieux Fort.

Chak Chak

Map 1, F14. Beanfield, Vieux
Fort ☏454-6260. Daily: lunch &
dinner. **Inexpensive to
moderate.**

Set amid a development of
resort cottages, this cheap and
cheerful joint often has live
music and the reasonable
prices attract patrons from

THE SOUTH COAST

nearby hotels. Rickety tables are set in a dark and sparsely decorated dining room or outside on the verandah and the menu, based around fresh fish, is serviceable. No credit cards.

Il Pirata
Map 1, F14. Vieux Fort ☎454-6610. Tues–Sun 7am–9.30pm. **Moderate.**
Dark Italian restaurant that isn't enhanced by a drab beachside setting near to the crumbling remnants of an old dock. The food, though, is a happy contrast; specialities include deep-oven pizza, home-made pastas and a decent fish Milanese. Also does breakfasts.

Juliette's Lodge
Map 1, F14. Beanfield, Vieux Fort ☎454-5300. Daily 7.30am–10pm. **Moderate.**
One of the better places to eat in Vieux Fort and popular with large groups. The basic fare of fried fish, pasta and steaks is tasty and swiftly served.

Reef Restaurant & Bar
Map 1, F14. Anse de Sables ☎454 3418. Tues–Sat 11am– late. **Inexpensive to moderate.**
A typical beachside restaurant and bar serving burgers, pizza and beer, along with some West Indian dishes. The best thing about it is the seashore location and there's also internet access and board games.

Sandy Beach Club
Map 1, F14. Anse de Sables ☎454-7416. Daily: lunch & dinner. **Moderate.**
On the sands at the southeast side of the airport, this beach bar and restaurant serves Creole dishes, burgers, sandwiches and exotic cocktails. It's one of the best places in Vieux Fort to eat, drink and relax by the ocean, though the opening hours are erratic – call ahead if you're planning on dinner.

THE SOUTH COAST

THE EAST

The scenery along the **east coast** is certainly picturesque, but you won't find many worthy restaurants along the way. As the coastline north of Dennery is pretty much inaccessible in anything other than a 4WD, there are no established restaurants.

Fox Grove Inn

Map 1, G9. Mon Repose ☎455-3271. Daily 8am–10pm, 12.30–2.30pm & 7–10pm. Moderate.

About ten minutes' drive from Vieux Fort, this lovely inn (see p.173) is a relaxing spot for alfresco lunches or special dinners, affording great views of the banana-and-cocoa clad hills, the Atlantic coastline and the protected Fregate Islands. Emphasis is on expertly prepared local produce, including a great selection of creative salads, and guaranteed-fresh fish from nearby Praslin Bay.

Manje Domi

Map 1, F11. Desruisseaux ☎455-0729. Daily 8am–11pm. Moderate.

An unexpected gem of a place in a small guesthouse (see p.174), serving tasty and filling Creole food with a focus on very fresh Atlantic fish and hearty or healthy local breakfasts. Both the restaurant and the cosy bar are popular with locals; call ahead to book.

Entertainment and nightlife

Though St Lucia isn't exactly the nightlife capital of the Caribbean, there's plenty to do after dark. Many hotels and restaurants in the west coast resort areas offer some sort of live music or dancing most nights of the week. Between Castries and Cap Estate, and particularly at Rodney Bay, there are numerous bars and restaurants where you can have a drink or a meal whilst listening to anything from a mellow jazz combo to the hotter licks of a reggae, calypso or steel pan band, or even traditional *chak-chak* groups and canned or live rock-and-roll. Karaoke is big at *The Lime* and the *Shamrock Pub* in Rodney Bay. Most pub-crawlers are a mix of young local people and tourists in search of dancing music, and if you're desperate for a dance floor, head for the in-house discos of larger hotels, where DJs spin the latest from North America and Europe. For more sedate entertainment, seek out the few jazz and piano bars.

Many of the larger resort hotels also offer their own evening **entertainment**, and non-guests are welcome unless the property is all-inclusive. This often consists of

ST LUCIAN MUSIC

The roots of **St Lucian music** go back to the days when slaves fashioned instruments from whatever materials came to hand, and the repertoire of local **folk music** began with work and game songs and festival and dance songs. Known by the name of their principal instrument, early musical groups centred around a rhythm instrument called a *chak-chak*, often a tin or hollowed-out log filled with seeds, while the *tambou* (a wooden drum with a goatskin head) beat time and a small banjo called a *banjo bwa payé* provided melody. Several groups keep the traditions alive today, playing at national events such as Carnival, Independence Day celebrations and the La Rose and La Marguerite festivals. The **vocals** that accompany the music are often improvized, with audience members tossing in a line here and there; like calypso, *chak-chak* music offers social and political commentary, often mixed with ribald lyrics. If you want to take home some traditional St Lucian music, the *Musical Traditions of St Lucia* compilation is a good bet; it's available from the Folk Research Centre in Castries (☎452-2279).

Modern popular music borrows from pan-Caribbean forms such as calypso, a favourite of Carnival, and soca, an upbeat dance music that mixes the storytelling tradition of calypso with the beat of America R&B. Reggae is also an island staple, and the frenetic sounds of *zouk*, a blend of funk, soca and African music which is popular in Martinique, Guadeloupe and other French islands, are guaranteed to fill the dance halls and discos.

seaside or poolside barbecues with steel bands or DJs playing, followed by those remarkably tacky **fire-eating** and **limbo dancing** shows that have become associated with the region despite the fact that fire-eating and limboing have nothing whatsoever to do with Caribbean people. The performances are more of a carnival sideshow than a cultural indicator, but they're fun if you relish a spectacle. As the bulk of in-hotel entertainment takes place during the high season, it's best to call ahead to see what's on.

The best source of current entertainment **information** is local newspapers and the tourist publication *Tropical Traveller*. You can always call establishments directly – numbers are provided with listings on the following pages.

St Lucia hosts several **regular events**, and two of the biggest in the annual entertainment calendar are the **St Lucia Jazz Festival** in May – four days of jazz, R&B and world music – and July's **Carnival**, celebrated with music, dance and parades and preceded by weeks of calypso contests and feasts. Lastly, a rundown on the entertainment scene must include the island's liveliest weekly event, the **Gros Islet Street Party**, or **jump-up**, held in the open air each Friday night and quite possibly St Lucia's most visited, and most famous, night-time attraction. Smaller (and friendlier) street parties, called **fish fries**, but incorporating rum, dancing and chat, take place in Anse La Raye on Friday and Dennery on Saturday nights, but the Gros Islet party is the biggest, brashest, latest and loudest of them all.

ST LUCIA JAZZ FESTIVAL

Since it commenced in 1991, the annual **St Lucia Jazz Festival** has made a splash on the international scene and has attracted some of the jazz and R&B worlds' biggest names, including Grover Washington, Herbie Hancock, Nancy Wilson, Mary J. Blige, Earl Klugh, Wynton Marsalis, the Neville Brothers, steel pan artist Boogsie Sharp, Chick Corea, Stanley Clarke, Wayne Shorter and George Benson. The four-day event takes place in early or mid-May at several venues, the main ones being Pigeon

Island and the Cultural Centre on the outskirts of Castries, while more intimate shows are held at an ever-changing, array of resorts, nightclubs and venues around the country, from Gros Islet to Vieux Fort. Many events are held outdoors at temporary stages erected for the shows, a wonderful way to combine the mellow energy of jazz with the relaxed tropical setting.

Some shows are free, such as the "Jazz in the Square" series held at Derek Walcott Square in Castries, but for most, you'll need to pay an entrance fee. **Tickets** for individual shows cost US$18–66 and are available from the *Jazz Shop* (℡ 451-8566, ℻ 452 5472) at Pointe Seraphine or via the **festival website** (Ⓦ www.stluciajazz.org) – you can book them before your visit and pick them up when you arrive. The festival attracts thousands of tourists and music aficionados, so if you want to attend, it's advisable to make airline and hotel reservations some months ahead to avoid disappointment.

The festival website has specific details about concerts and dates – you can even vote in advance for your favourite artist lineup and possibly win a free trip to the festival. General festival **information** is also available from the tourist board in St Lucia (℡ 452-4094) and from offices abroad (see p.22).

For a full list of St Lucia's festivals
and public holidays, see pp.49–52.

CARNIVAL

An island-wide round of dancing, street masquerading, competitive calypsoing, feasting and general partying, St Lucia's **Carnival** is one of the true showcases of the island's culture, with storytelling, folk dancing and traditional music

CARNIVAL

such as *chak-chak* bands afforded as much prominence as the more contemporary Carnival melee of sequinned bikinis and thumping soca music. It's kid-friendly, too, with lots of children's costume parades and special events such as the Junior Carnival King and Queen contests. Major events, such as opening, crowning and closing ceremonies and the main parades, usually take places around Derek Walcott Square or Mindoo Philip Park – usually a cricket ground – in Castries.

While it might not seem so from the revelry that surrounds the event, Carnival has distinctly non-secular roots, having evolved amongst Catholics as a last fling before the austerity of Lent. In the Caribbean and further afield, the tradition gradually became Africanized, an opportunity for slaves to let loose and parody their owners with overblown costumes, music and dance traditions from their native lands. However, in an attempt to attract more tourists, and to avoid coinciding with other popular Caribbean Carnivals (particularly that of Trinidad), the 1999 event was shifted from the original pre-Lenten dates to the first half of July and will remain that way indefinitely. Many believe the move to July has erased the true meaning of the festival and that Carnival will become just another tourist-oriented activity.

Carnival **information** is available from the tourist board in St Lucia (℡ 452-4094), from offices abroad (see pp.21–22) and at ⓦ www.stluciacarnival.com.

THEATRE

You can catch shows at various venues around the country, notably the **Derek Walcott Theatre**, a small open-air amphitheatre adjacent to the *Great House* restaurant in the Cap Estate hills (℡ 450-0450). The theatre showcases local playwrights and actors, and the plays are well worth seeing

THEATRE

for their insights into local culture as well as for their literary value. Nobel Prize-winner Walcott (see box on p.61) is the inspiration for local writers and he was instrumental in the theatre's development; his own work is also occasionally staged. Plays are in English or in Patois (not easy to understand) and range in theme and presentation from broad farce to serious drama. In general, St Lucians are not theatre-going folk, but the Castries crowd like to turn out for performances. Tickets start at about EC$10.

Also well worth checking out are the excellent singing and dancing performances by **Folk Research Centre** groups (☎452-2279). The centre, on L'Anse Road in Castries' Morne Pleasant, presents their traditional, non-touristy productions year round, but the bulk of performances are staged around Carnival time.

GROS ISLET STREET PARTY

Completely overtaking the village of Gros Islet, the popular Friday night **street party** (also known as the **jump-up** or, locally, as plain old **Friday Night**) is the highlight of St Lucia's weekly nightlife schedule. The festivities are fairly self-explanatory: from around 10pm, the streets are packed with revellers dancing, drinking and feasting on barbecued food sold by hordes of enterprising vendors. Dauphine Street and its surrounds are closed to traffic, the bars are wide open, and the reggae, soca and calypso music blasts from all angles.

For more on the Gros Islet street party, see p.87.

It can be great fun, but a word of caution – of late, the party has started to attract vendors peddling marijuana and even sex alongside the fried chicken, and reports of crime suggest that it's sensible to leave valuables back at the hotel and bring with you only what you'll need to spend. Women should expect to be approached by aggressively interested (and sometimes overly persistent) men; for tips on how best to deal with this kind of attention, see p.44.

BARS AND LIVE MUSIC

The St Lucian **bar scene** is at its liveliest in Castries and Rodney Bay. Most drinking spots and hotel bars offer some sort of enticement to get people in, such as 5–7pm **happy hours** with two-for-one deals on drinks. **Ladies' nights** are also a draw, with free admission or reduced drinks prices for women. There are no set **licensing hours** in St Lucia, and most establishments will stay open as long as there are customers. Cover charges for the **live music** shows held in bars and pubs start at around US$5 per person.

CASTRIES AND AROUND

Beach Facilities
Map 3, D5. Vigie Beach
℡ 452-5494.
This small, dark bar on Vigie beach offers cheap eats and the odd performance by live bands on weekends. With the waves lapping the shore, it's a pleasant place for a drink even after the sun goes down.

The Wharf Beach Bar
Map 3, F3. Choc Bay ℡ 451-3000.

This beachside restaurant lays on occasional live music – look out for family nights and other theme evenings, as well as the regular Tuesday night karaoke songfest.

GROS ISLET AND THE NORTH

Indies
Map 4, G9. Rodney Bay
℡ 452-0727.
Attracting a lively mix of locals and visitors and upscale in its own way – proper dress is required, meaning no

beach wear – *Indies* puts on busy theme nights; the popular Wednesday "Beach Bash" provides drinks, music and round-trip transport from your hotel for one price (US$15). Friday and Saturday are often Ladies' Nights, when women get free drinks.

The Jazz Lounge
Map 4, E8. Rodney Bay
☎ 453-6294.

St Lucia's only jazz café opens at 8pm with a one-hour happy hour before shows, and offers tapas and late night dining as well as a fine wine menu until 1.30am. Local and Caribbean jazz artists play here and dancing is positively encouraged. The separate *Roof Garden* (see p.186) restaurant is upstairs.

La Creole
Map 4, G8. Rodney Bay
☎ 450-0022.

This popular seafood restaurant on the strip of land between the Castries–Gros Islet Highway and the Rodney Bay Marina has night-time salsa and disco

dancing and occasional live music such as oldies bands or *zouk* from the French West Indies. Popular with tourists and locals alike.

The Lime
Map 4, E8. Rodney Bay
☎ 452-0282.

Most nights, you'll hear a lone singer with guitar in the streetside courtyard of *The Lime* – clap for him once in a while, he's looking for it. The restaurant's disco next door, *Late Lime*, is open Wednesday, Friday and Saturday for dancing to a wide range of live music and sometimes hosts comedy acts. This is one of the island's hottest nightlife venues, likely to be crowded with young St Lucians and tourists feverishly dancing the night away.

Razmataz
Map 4, E7. Rodney Bay
☎ 452-9800.

The *Razmataz* serves East Indian fare and has live music on selected evenings and a belly dancer on Saturday nights.

BARS AND LIVE MUSIC

Shamrock's Pub

Map 4, E8. Rodney Bay
☎452-8725.

On the Rodney Bay waterfront, *Shamrock's* is a rocking place, and with something going on just about every night, it's bound to be crowded. On Monday you can get big pitchers of beer for about EC\$15, Tuesday is Ladies' Night, when women get two-for-one drinks (though rumour has it that some of the "ladies" are less than desirable company), and from Wednesday to Sunday there are theme nights, sometimes featuring live music and with karaoke on Thursday evenings. Also on hand are pool tables and table football games.

Triangle Pub

Map 4, E8. Rodney Bay
☎452-0334.

Small barbecue next to *The Lime* which puts on live music every night, from reggae and steel bands to jazz. Great fun, and great food, too.

SOUFRIÈRE AND THE WEST COAST

JJ's

Map 1, D6. Marigot Bay Road
☎451-4076.

On the road to the bay, *JJ's* runs a popular Seafood Night on Wednesday, with dancing to all sorts of music afterward. Local opposition has meant that his late week-night parties have come to an end, but there is still some form of entertainment most nights of the week.

THE SOUTH AND EAST COASTS

Club Zodiak

Map 1, F14. Beanfield Cottages, Beanfield, Vieux Fort
☎454-6260.

Set in the *Beanfield Cottages* complex, next to the *Chak-Chak* restaurant, this makeshift disco is actually a small room with what appears to be aluminium foil plastered on the walls. There is live music at the weekends during the high season; otherwise, the DJs take over with loud reggae, rap and *zouk*. The crowd is made up of mostly young St Lucians letting loose.

The Reef
Map 1, F14. Anse de Sables, Vieux Fort ☎454-7416.

Live music and dancing on the beach during high-season weekends for a predominantly young crowd of tourists, locals and students from a nearby medical school. During the off season, call to find out if there's anything happening.

Sports and other activities

With miles of easily accessible sandy beaches and the vast ocean never more than a couple of miles away, St Lucia is perfect for watersports. Larger resort hotels often have their own watersports facilities, usually snorkelling, scuba diving, sea kayaking, windsurfing and sailing on small, single-sail one- or two-person Sunfish boats. Some places also have their own yachts, often catamarans, for sunset and snorkelling excursions, as well as fishing trips. Except at all-inclusives, non-guests can usually use in-hotel facilities – for a fee, of course.

If no watersports are on offer where you're staying and you don't want to use the facilities at other hotels, look out for the numerous privately run outfits at St Lucia's marinas and the more popular beaches. In the **north** of the island, the best places to start are the Vigie Marina in Castries and the Rodney Bay Marina near Rodney Bay town. The Moorings Marina at **Marigot Bay** is a good bet if you're staying in the area; and in the **south**, try the waterfront in Soufrière, where several fishing boats and excursion yachts dock.

ST LUCIA'S BEST BEACHES

St Lucia, quite rightfully, is lauded for the variety of its beaches, ranging from dark patches of volcanic sand teeming with marine life in Soufrière to golden stretches of sun worshippers' delight in the north. Reduit Beach at Rodney Bay is the most popular – and crowded – of the northern beaches, although the stretches of sand just north, around the *LeSPORT* resort and Cap Estate, are more stunning and private. For those looking for more than just sun, the beach at Anse Chastanet and the neighbouring Anse Mamin attract scuba divers and snorkellers, while windsurfers enjoy the swelling wind and waves of Anse de Sables, near Vieux Fort in the south. Sea turtle fans can join a turtle watch to Grand Anse, a gorgeous beach on the island's Atlantic side – for more details see p.136.

Visitors should be aware that the waters around the North East of the island are very powerful and unsuitable for swimming – both locals and tourists have died here. Furthermore, all beaches on St Lucia are public, so while you might feel pressured into renting a sun lounger (usually around US$10– $25/day) at some of the fancier resorts, you are under no obligation to do so. Note that nude and topless bathing are illegal on the island.

Beaches on the west coast are generally calm and safe for **swimming**, but some in the east have dangerous rough spots, easily recognizable by the crashing surf which often indicates strong undertows. Ask local advice and go in only up to your knees if you're not a strong swimmer. The waters surrounding the island are pretty clean, but unconfirmed reports suggest that Reduit Beach and Rodney Bay may harbour some **pollution**. In most cases, swimming in rivers and waterfalls is safe, though you should take your cue from locals. Try to swim upstream, as the closer a river gets to the coast, the more likely it is to be polluted.

There's plenty to do out of the water as well. Easily accessible land-based sports include **tennis**, **squash**, **golf**, and **horseback riding**; larger hotels often have **gyms** as well – there are also a couple of privately run operators in Gablewoods Mall. While many of the more sizeable hotels have tennis courts (and, again, allow non-guests to use them for a fee), there are also several public courts with good facilities – some of these also have resident pros who can provide lessons. St Lucia has one public golf course at Cap Estate, though it's likely to be crowded during week-ends in the busy winter season.

Wilderness lovers who like to explore will find a good number of **hiking trails** in the island's interior forest reserves, as well as along the east coast, which allow visitors to get close to St Lucia's diverse flora and fauna.

SCUBA DIVING

St Lucia's **diving** is not as highly regarded as the region's more pristine scuba environments, such as Saba or Bonaire. Visibility is generally fair, but rivers spilling into the ocean at places such as Soufrière and Vieux Fort bays can muddy the vistas. Still, many of the reefs – particularly in the south around the base of the Pitons – are excellent dive sites, and there are several submerged wrecks to explore.

If you've never tried scuba diving, it's easy to learn in St Lucia by taking a PADI (Professional Association of Diving Instructors) beginners' training course. Known as **resort courses**, these take you through the basics (usually in a swimming pool), before heading to the ocean for a super-vized dive of about forty feet (12m). Costs start at US$80. If you're interested (and have both the time and the money), more detailed certification programmes such as open water, advanced open water and refresher courses are available from various dive centres for US$200–450. These generally include daily dive fees, manuals, dive tables, a log book and certification processing fees, and sometimes equipment.

If you have **certification**, you should of course bring along your card as well as any pieces of equipment you'd rather not rent. Some operators include diving gear in their packages, so it's worth checking beforehand. If you're certified, **prices** start at about US$50 for a one-tank dive, with night dives costing from US$70. Packages for multiple dives start at US$120 for four dives over two days and go up to as much as US$280 for ten dives in five days. If you're a serious enthusiast, it might be worth looking into packages offered by hotels such as *Anse Chastanet*, *Still Beach Resort* and the *Marigot Beach Club*, which bundle flights, accommodation and a specified number of dives at ostensibly discounted rates – however, deals vary, and it's worth checking the specifics before you book.

SNORKELLING

Snorkelling is particularly good around the island's south-western fringes, where the **Soufrière Marine Management Area** (see p.105) hugs the shoreline for nearly seven miles from Anse L'Ivrogne south of Gros Piton to Anse Jambon, just north of Anse Chastanet. The reefs here are pristine by most standards, and the area is protected for fishing and recreational use; the nominal dive fee (US$3 per day or US$10 per year) goes toward the park's upkeep. Areas around the base of Petit Piton and Anse Chastanet bay are particularly stunning places to snorkel. The main **coral varieties** in St Lucian waters include the sizeable, tan-coloured elkhorn, pale yellow or white finger coral, rotund brain coral and the soft gorgonian type, coloured purple or green. **Fish** are plentiful and the most frequent reef visitors are angelfish (blue and yellow

WATERSPORTS OPERATORS

Buddies Scuba Rodney Bay, Castries ☎452-9086, Ⓦwww
.superior.co.uk/buddies. Scuba and snorkelling.

Club Mistral Anse de Sables, Vieux Fort ☎454-3418,
Ⓦwww.club-mistral.com. Windsurfing.

Dive Fair Helen Vigie Cove, ☎451-7716, Ⓦwww.divefairhelen
.com. Snorkelling and scuba diving, with special accommo-
dation/dive packages available with *Ti Kaye Resort* and
Wyndham Morgan Bay.

Dolphin Divers Rodney Bay ☎452-9482. Scuba and
snorkelling.

Frog's Diving *Still Plantation & Beach Resort*, Soufrière ☎452-
8331; *Windjammer Landing*, Labrellotte Bay ☎452-8331;
Ⓦwww.frogsdiving.com. Scuba and snorkelling.

Marigot Dive Resort Marigot Bay ☎451-4974, Ⓦwww.marigot
diveresort.com. Scuba, snorkelling, sailing, windsurfing, kayaking.

Scuba St Lucia *Anse Chastanet*, Soufrière ☎459-7755 or 459-
7000, Ⓦwww.scubastlucia.com. Scuba and snorkelling.

with darkish stripes), red squirrelfish, bright blue parrotfish,
green or blue and yellow wrasses and the triggerfish, dark
green with a yellow belly and an elongated snout.

Many of the island's diving centres rent masks and fins for
about US$10 per hour and will also take you out for an
escorted offshore trip, often a far more rewarding option
than striking out alone from the beach. Trips cost
US$20–35, including equipment and a guide who will take
you to the best snorkel spots and point out things of interest.

BOAT TRIPS

Gliding up and down St Lucia's accessible and calm west
coast, **sightseeing** and **party boats** (usually customized

catamarans) offer a great way to see the bays and interior mountain peaks from a different perspective. Most excursions include stops for snorkelling and swimming, or a visit to a coastal village (probably Soufrière or Marigot Bay) as well as lunch and drinks. However, you should bear in mind that as the boats are often crowded with rowdy revellers taking advantage of the free-flowing rum, the trip may not be the quiet cruise you anticipated; if you're looking for a more sedate excursion, say so when you book. Most trips depart from Vigie Marina in Castries or the Rodney Bay Marina and head south along the coast for full- or half-day cruises, which start at US$75 per person for the full day and about US$40 for the half day; check whether transport to and from your hotel is included in the price.

One of the best **cruise operators** is Endless Summer Cruises (℡ 450-8651, Ⓦ www.endlesssummer.net), which runs full-day tours out of Rodney Bay to Soufrière's volcano and Diamond Falls, with stops at beaches around Anse Cochon for swimming and snorkelling, as well as sightseeing at Marigot Bay. They also operate half-day swimming jaunts to various spots along the northwest coast. Used in the filming of the movie *Roots*, the *Unicorn* (℡ 452-6811, Ⓦ www.brigunicorn.com) is a 140-foot brig that looks like an old pirate ship and makes trips to Soufrière and the surrounding attractions, while the *Mango Tango* catamaran (℡ 452-0459) takes snorkellers out to various west coast spots. For a larger, all-inclusive tour that takes in Soufrière's active volcano and the Diamond waterfall and botanical gardens, with lunch at *Still Plantation*, call Sunlink Tours (℡ 452-8232).

WINDSURFING

For those into **windsurfing**, Club Mistral (daily 9am–10pm, ℡ 454-3418, Ⓦ www.club-mistral.com) at

Anse de Sables offers courses and equipment for beginners and experts alike. The water at Anse de Sables is noted for its excellent windsurfability, and the area was the subject of a recent BBC documentary on the sport.

YACHT CHARTERS

Sailing around St Lucia or visiting neighbouring islands aboard your own private yacht has become increasingly popular in recent years, and several companies in St Lucia will **charter a yacht**. Costs depend on the size of the group the length of time you'll be sailing and the size of the yacht, but you can expect to pay anywhere from US$1400 per week in low season to US$6100 per week in high season. If you don't have sailing skills or you're after complete relaxation (and no work), a captain and crew or a cook can accompany you, but this will add considerably to the costs: a captain is roughly US$100 per day, a cook about US$60 per day and a crew US$25–30 each per day. The larger charter companies can arrange complete packages that base your holiday around yachting and include charter fees, airfares and hotel stays while the boat is prepared. The most reliable operators include: **Destination St Lucia** (Rodney Bay ☎452-8531, ⓦwww.dsl-yachting.com), **Moorings Yacht Charters** (Marigot Bay ☎451-4230; in North America ☎888/922-☎4811; ⓦwww.moorings.com) and **Stirrup Yachts** (Castries ☎452-8000).

SPORT FISHING

Sport fishing enthusiasts will find good game fishing offshore of St Lucia, where the main catches include sizeable marlin, kingsfish, wahoo and shark. If you're lucky, you might also hook the rarer tuna, dorado or mackerel. Deep-sea fishing excursions run half or full days, with bait and tackle (and sometimes drinks) included; full-day trips include lunch. Half-days start at about US$300 for as many as six people. To arrange a trip, contact Hackshaw's at Castries (☎ 453-0553), Captain Mike at Vigie Marina (☎ 452-7044) or Mako Watersports at Rodney Bay (☎ 452-0412).

GYMS AND SPAS

When it's time to work off all that Creole conch and rum punch, head for St Lucia's best **gym**, Sportivo at Rodney Heights (☎ 452-8899). Also on the island are: Body Inc. at the Gablewoods Mall (☎ 451-9744), owned by former Mr Universe and current politician and media magnate, Rick Wayne; Mango Moon Total Fitness at Lunar Park, Vigie Marina (☎ 453-1934); The St Lucia Racquet Club (☎ 450-0551); and Doolittle's Gym in Marigot Bay (☎ 451-4974). Most are well-equipped with free weights, a good selection of brand-name units and aerobics equipment such as treadmills and offer a variety of fitness classes daily. Entrance requires temporary membership – a rather hefty US$25 per day, US$80 per day for a family, with rates by the week or month.

After you've worked your body to a pulp, you can let someone else work to soothe it. The Royal Spa (☎ 452-9999) at the *Royal St Lucian* resort in Rodney Bay (see p.162) is open daily to non-guests for a wide range of **spa treatments**, from aromatherapy massages to facials and mud wraps. They also have a well-equipped fitness centre and a whirlpool bath and sauna. Treatments are charged on an individual basis and range from US$10 for an hour and a half in the sauna, to a pricey US$105 for hydrotherapy. Services are also available at *LeSPORT* hotel's Oasis spa (☎ 450-8551) and are somewhat cheaper than the *Royal*, starting at around US$40 for a one-hour massage, US$25 for a facial. Other services include salt loofah rubs and seaweed wraps.

TENNIS AND SQUASH

Tennis is on offer at most hotels for as little as US$5 per hour and the St Lucia Racquet Club (℡450–0551) has nine floodlit courts for night games – tennis is free for guests, and EC$25 per day for visitors; racquet rental is EC$20 per hour. Jalousie Hilton (℡459–7666) has four courts open to visitors, three lit for night play, and charges non-guests EC$25 per hour. St Lucia Yacht Club in Rodney Bay (℡452–8350) will let non-members use its squash courts for a fee of EC$10 per hour.

BIKING

Mountain biking is available at Anse Mamin, a small, secluded beach accessible only from Anse Chastanet beach (ask at the Scuba St Lucia shop for a free lift) or by hired boat from the Soufrière shore. Here, set in several miles of rainforest, there are custom-built off-road trails ranging from beginner – suitable for families – to damn impossible (you try to conquer Tinker's Trail). The operators, Bike St Lucia (℡459–7755, ⓦwww.bikestlucia.com), ensure that you know how to handle their professional bikes before letting you loose for the day to explore the trails and enjoy the eighteenth-century French plantation ruins, fresh-water reservoir and swimming hole, not to mention the stunning snorkelling on deserted Anse Mamin beach. Bikes are new, staff are professional and this is a heartily recommended day out. Bike St Lucia offer a full day taxi/boat package from any hotel in the north of the island for US$75 per person; if you make your own way to the beach at Anse Chastanet, the cost is US$49 per day.

HORSEBACK RIDING

Horseback riding is a great way to see the country, particularly the mountains or east coast where roads are poor and access by car is difficult. Most stables provide lessons as well as one- to four-hour rides, with transport to and from your hotel and possibly lunch included. Rides cost US$25–40 per hour.

In the **Gros Islet** area, try Trim's (℡ 450-8273) or North Point (℡ 450-8853); in the **south**, contact Trekkers at Morne Coubaril Estate in Soufrière (℡ 459-7340).

GOLF

The St Lucia Golf and Country Club in Cap Estate (℡ 450-8523, ⓦ www.stluciagolf.com) is the island's first and only eighteen-hole **public golf course**, a par 71, and while it's not bad, it can get a little soggy during the rainy season. Greens fees are US$95 for eighteen holes, US$70 for nine holes; golf club rental costs US$20, shoes US$10. Lessons are available from the club pro and cost from US$40 for thirty minutes. Alternatively, the all-inclusive *Sandals St Lucia* hotel in La Toc (℡ 452-3081) allows non-guests to play their nine-hole, par-33 course for a fee of around US$20 for eighteen holes.

HIKING

Hiking through St Lucia's central rainforests and reserves is the best way to experience the island's fabulously beautiful **interior**; despite being laced by walkable trails, the mountains often go unexplored by beach devotees. You don't necessarily need guides for many of the hikes (though hiring one will help to identify local flora and fauna), but you do need advance permission from the Department of Forest and Lands (☎450-2231, ⓦww.slumaffe.org/forestry to enter protected areas such as the Edmund Forest Reserve, Des Cartiers Rainforest and the Barre de L'Isle area. Rangers, who serve as guides, are found at the trailheads, and there is a fee (see Chapter 6).

Walks on off-shore **coastal reserves** such as the Fregate and Maria islands, as well as tours of the Morne Fortune historic area in Castries, are conducted by the St Lucia National Trust, who you can call for times and costs (☎452-5005; see also p.123).

If you decide to hike, bear in mind that you'll be doing so in the tropical heat; wear light clothing and bring a hat, sunscreen and plenty of water. Sneakers are fine if you don't have walking shoes or boots, but be aware that paths can be extremely steep, and are slippery after rains. For more on hiking practicalities, see p.139.

Directory

Airlines in St Lucia Air Canada ⓣ 452-2550; Air Jamaica ⓣ 453-6611; Air Martinique ⓣ 452-2463 or 453-6660; American Airlines ⓣ 454-6777; American Eagle ⓣ 452-1820; BWIA ⓣ 452-3778 or 452-3789; LIAT ⓣ 452-3051.

Banks Castries: Bank of Nova Scotia (Scotiabank), William Peter Blvd and High St/Chausee Rd; Barclays, Bridge St; Caribbean Banking Corporation, Micoud St; CIBC, William Peter Blvd; National Commercial Bank, Bridge St and waterfront; Royal Bank of Canada, William Peter Blvd; St Lucia Cooperative Bank, Bridge St. **Sunny Acres**: Caribbean Banking Corporation, Gablewoods Mall. **Rodney Bay Marina**: Bank of Nova Scotia (Scotiabank), Barclays, National Commercial Bank, Royal Bank of Canada, St Lucia Cooperative Bank, JQ's Shopping Mall. **Soufrière**: Barclays, Bridge St; National Commercial Bank, Bridge St. **Vieux Fort**: Bank of Nova Scotia (Scotiabank), New Dock Rd; Barclays, Bridge St; Caribbean Banking Association, Gablewoods South; National Commercial Bank, Clarke St; CIBC, Clarke St; Royal Bank of Canada, New Dock Rd.

Customs You are allowed a duty-free quota of one litre of spirits or wine, 200 cigarettes, 50 cigars and 250g of tobacco on arrival in St Lucia. The first EC$250 in gifts brought in (which includes the spirits and tobacco, but not personal effects) is not subject to duty charges. It goes without saying that attempting to bring illegal drugs into St Lucia incurs severe penalties. For questions, call Customs ☏ 454-6509. For customs information regarding your country of origin, contact the proper local authorities.

Departure tax Departure tax is EC$54 (US$22) per person, payable at the airport. Try to have the exact sum as ticket-counter personnel do not always have change in currencies other than EC dollars.

Electricity The standard is 220 volts, although many hotels have 110-volt systems. There will sometimes be a limited number of adapters for use by guests, but it's best to bring one yourself if you think you'll need it.

Embassies and Consulates British High Commission, 2nd Floor, Sir Stanislaus James Building, Waterfront, Castries ☏ 452-2484. The US, Australia and Canada are represented in Barbados. US Consulate: American Life Insurance

Company (ALICO) building, Cheapside, Bridgetown ☏ 1-246/431-0225. Australian High Commission: Bishop's Court Hill, St Michael ☏ 1-809/435-2834. Canadian High Commission: Lower Collymore Rock St, St Michael ☏ 1-246/429-3550. New Zealand is not represented in the region.

Emergencies For police dial ☏ 999, for fire and ambulance dial ☏ 911.

Gay and lesbian St Lucia While direct animosity is unlikely, St Lucia is one of the more backward islands in the Caribbean in its approach to gay visitors. Some resorts may tolerate gay couples, others – including the *Sandals* chain – specify heterosexual couples only. In general, you're best sticking to the smaller guesthouses and hotels, amongst which there are three specifically gay-friendly establishments: the self-catering *Seascape* (see p.158), the lovely, small *Hotel CAPri* (see p.164) at Cap Estate and the *Inn on the Bay* guesthouse (see p.166), in Marigot Bay.

Hospitals Victoria Hospital in Castries (☎452-2421) is the island's main public facility and has a 24-hour emergency room. The private Tapion Hospital (☎459-2000) is on La Toc Rd south of the city. In Vieux Fort, call private teaching hospital St Judes (☎454-6684). There are smaller **medical centres** at Soufrière (☎459-7258) and Dennery (☎453-3310).

Laundries Hotel laundries are expensive, charging as much as US$2–5 for short-sleeved shirts and US$3–6 for long pants or skirts. The self-service machines at U Wash N Dry on Darling St in Castries (☎451-7664) are less expensive. You can also drop off washing at So White Cleaners on Marie Therese St in Gros Islet (☎450-8808) or in the laundromat in Gablewoods Mall.

Library Each town has a small library, but the largest is the Central Library (☎452-2875) on Derek Walcott Square in Castries. Hours vary, but most open from Monday to Saturday between 10am and 1pm; several branches remain open until 6pm on selected days. To borrow books, visitors must leave a cash deposit of EC$40, which is refunded when books are returned.

Measurements St Lucia is gradually switching from imperial to metric. Some road signs are in miles, others in kilometres; petrol is sold by the litre but fishermen weigh and sell their catch by the pound.

Pharmacies In and around **Castries**, try Clarke and Company, Bridge St (☎452-2727), Williams on Bridge St (☎452 2792), Rose Medical Centre on Micoud St (☎452-3333) or Minvielle & Chastanet, Gablewoods Mall (☎451-7808). Clarke and Company also have a branch on Bridge St in **Soufrière**, and at JQ's Plaza in **Vieux Fort** (☎454-3761). Minvielle & Chastanet also have a Vieux Fort shop on New Dock Rd (☎454-3760) and at JQ's Shopping Mall (☎458-0178). Most branches of Clarke and Company open on weekdays from 8am until 4pm and until 12.30pm on Saturdays; Minvielle & Chastanet open

●

from 8am to 6pm weekdays and from 9am to 1pm on Saturdays.

Photography Prints and slides can be **developed** at Cadet's on Hospital Rd, south of downtown Castries (☎453-1446); they offer one-hour processing, as do Foto 1 Club on High St in Castries (☎453-0514), which also sells photographic supplies. Quality is usually good, but you'll pay more than at home. If you want to photograph St Lucian people, ask permission first.

Time St Lucia is on Atlantic Standard Time, four hours behind Greenwich Mean Time and one hour ahead of Eastern Standard Time. No seasonal adjustments are made.

Tipping and taxes Hotels add a ten percent service charge and an eight percent government tax on room charges, which may be included in the rates or added on to your final bill (see p.152). Restaurants often add a ten percent service charge, though feel free to add a further tip. Hotel porters and taxi

drivers have come to expect ten to fifteen percent tips.

Tour operators Probably the easiest way to go if you want to organize something more complicated than a simple day trip. In **Castries**, try Cox & Co on William Peter Blvd (☎452-2211), or M & C Tourist Development on Bridge St (☎458-8283); in **Gros Islet** call Barefoot Holidays, Gros Islet Industrial Estate (☎450-0507); and on Reduit Beach Avenue in **Rodney Bay**, contact Sunlink Tours (☎452-8232, ⓦwww.stluciareps.com).

Travel agents Local travel agents can be useful for booking tours around the island, scheduling trips to neighbouring islands or reconfirming flights. In **Castries**, there are many such agents on Micoud Street – try Carib Travel (☎452-2151), International Travel Consultants (☎452-3131) or St Lucia International Travel Services (☎452-1293); alternatively contact Barnard's Travel (☎452-2214) or Solar Tours and Travel (☎452-5898) on Bridge St, or

Hibiscus Travel on Bourbon St (☏ 453-1527). In **Rodney Bay**, go with Spice Travel (☏ 452-0865).

Water St Lucia's tap water is good and safe to drink, but can be in very short supply in the dry summer months. Inexpensive bottled water is available from larger supermarkets and most hotels.

Weddings To get married in St Lucia, you must bring the originals of your passport, birth certificate and appropriate documentation if either partner has been divorced or is a widow/widower. Once on St Lucia, you must appoint a local solicitor to apply for a marriage licence, which will be issued after you have been on the island for two days; the application takes two business days to process, so in effect you will not be married until the fifth day after you apply. Total fees for getting married in St Lucia, including lawyer, licence, notary's fees, marriage officer and certificate, amount to around US$300, more for extras like *chak chak* bands, music, photographs or a video.

CONTEXTS

A brief history of St Lucia

S t Lucia's first known inhabitants were the peaceful Arawaks, a race of fishermen and farmers who arrived from South America around 200 AD aboard dugout canoes. They settled in fertile plains adjacent to the sea or to rivers where they planted tobacco (which was used ritually), maize, cassava (the starchy staple of the tropics, which they called yuca), and guava, used as both a medicine and a food. Arawak paintings, or petroglyphs, have been found around Soufrière, the south and the southeast coasts of St Lucia, suggesting that these were the main areas in which the Arawaks settled; their language has also survived in words still used today, such as canoe, guava, barbecue, manatee and hurricane – "tobacco" is derived from the Arawak word for a pipe.

The Arawaks' life on St Lucia was relatively stable until the arrival, between 800 and 1200 AD, of the bellicose **Caribs**, another seagoing group from South America who made their way up the Lesser Antilles chain in war canoes, capturing and destroying entire Arawak villages, murdering the men and making off with the women. The Caribs named St Lucia *Iouanalao* (also spelled *Iyanola*) or "Land of Iguanas", which later evolved to *Hiwanarau* and finally to Hewanorra, now employed as the name of the island's international airport. By the late fifteenth century, when the first European explorers arrived in the Caribbean, St Lucia had been inhabited by Caribs for over 200 years, and by the early sixteenth century, Caribs had driven off or slaughtered most of the island's Arawak population. The aggressive Carib presence dominated the region and their reputation was far-reaching enough for the Spanish to name the entire Caribbean Sea after them. Carib hostility had become the chief hindrance to European settlement of the Caribbean and their barbarian reputation is probably behind the unproven assertion that they *ate* their adversaries.

European discovery and settlement

Unlike most other Caribbean islands, the European "discovery" of St Lucia is an ambiguous matter. Though it was long assumed that **Christopher Columbus** must have sighted St Lucia on his fourth and final voyage in 1502, no references to the island exist in his records, and it's unlikely that he ever saw St Lucia, let alone landed there. The island's name refers to St Lucie, an Italian saint whose feast day is December 13, and though this date was celebrated as "Discovery Day" for years, Columbus's logs indicate that he was nowhere near St Lucia on that day. It's most likely, though, that the first European to sight the island was indeed a Spaniard. Juan de la Cosa had sailed with Columbus on his first two voyages, and during an independent expedition of 1504, he sighted St Lucia and named it El Falcón on the maps he prepared. In 1511, the island appeared on a Spanish Royal Cedula of Population as St Lucia, and was included on a Vatican map of 1520.

As they did with many other islands in the region, the

Spanish claimed St Lucia in absentia soon after de la Cosa's visit, but their attempts to establish settlements were swiftly repelled by the Caribs and they made no great effort to colonize the island. In 1600, the **Dutch** made an abortive attempt to develop St Lucia as a reprovisioning stop-off for ships heading to the Americas or exploring the region. Their small **defence position** at the town now called Vieux Fort was destroyed by the Caribs and they were expeditiously driven from the island.

The next Europeans to arrive on St Lucian shores did so by accident: in 1605, a **British** ship called the *Olive Branch* was blown off course on its way to Guyana, and its 67 settlers were forced to land on the south coast of St Lucia. Soon after negotiating with the Caribs for shelter, the settlers were attacked. A prolonged battle followed and five weeks later the nineteen surviving settlers escaped in Carib canoes. In 1639, a British group under the command of one Sir Thomas Warner arrived, but within two years, they too had been driven off. Similar clashes between Caribs and small bands of settlers continued for another dozen years, during which time the **French** were busy building up their Caribbean presence and were able to claim St Lucia alongside several neighbouring islands with little opposition. They also established the **French West India Company**, a profit-making enterprise charged with regulating French mercantile enterprises in the New World.

French settlement and British challenge

The French West India Company often sub-chartered islands in its possession, and in 1651, St Lucia was **sold** to Governor du Parquet of neighbouring Martinique, who built a bastion on the peninsula to the north of Castries now called Vigie. The French made their settlement along a small creek that emptied into the bay at Vigie, that they called Le Carenage, and continued to battle with the Caribs until a **peace agreement** was signed in 1660. The cessation of Carib hostility allowed the French to consolidate their presence on St Lucia, but at the same time, the British were attempting to assert their supremacy throughout the region and ownership of St Lucia became part of the wider battle to gain control of Caribbean islands. Over the next 150 years, prolonged and bloody Anglo–French **hostilities** saw the "Helen of the West Indies" change hands fourteen times.

The Caribs were also caught up in the struggle for sovereignty over St Lucia: both the French and the British used Carib aggression to their advantage by employing them as **mercenaries**. At the same time, British and French **missionaries** were making great efforts to convert Caribs from their perceived heathen beliefs to Christianity. Nonconformers were often killed and systematic annihilation (as well as mass suicides) continued until the Caribs could offer no further resistance, whereupon the British (during one of their periods of power) gathered most of them up and shipped them off to a reservation in Dominica, which remains the last bastion of true Caribs in the Caribbean.

In spite of the fighting, the French made the first concerted efforts to turn St Lucia into a money-making colony around this time, settling along the fertile southeast coast and establishing a **town** that they called Soufrière in 1743, and officially designating it the capital in 1746. By 1765, they had introduced **sugar cane**, setting up vast plantations and bringing in **slaves** from West Africa to tend the crops that they hoped would earn them huge profits. However, the British offensives throughout the next century prevented the sugar industry from becoming the major enterprise it was on nearby islands such as Barbados.

The British and the Brigands wage war

In retaliation for French support of the fledgling colonies in America's War of Independence, the British initiated a prolonged attack against the French in 1778. After four years of fighting, Britain's **Admiral George Rodney** had established a bastion and a regional base for British ships at Pigeon Island, and from here he launched an attack on French naval forces stationed at the nearby Iles des Saintes archipelago off the coast of Guadeloupe. The French navy was decimated, and British victory in what became known as the **Battle of the Saints** signified that French domination of the Caribbean was soon to end.

For more on Admiral Rodney, see p.85.

However, French control of St Lucia was not immediately relinquished. The 1783 Treaty of Paris put St Lucia into French hands once again, and the effect of the 1789–99 French Revolution was felt on the island when Republicans changed the face of St Lucia. All the towns were renamed, French nobles were executed by **guillotine** and, in a radical move of solidarity, the Republicans **freed the slaves**. Noting the disarray caused by the revolution and sensing that the British would soon regain power, the Africans justly feared for their new-found freedom. While many stayed on the plantations, others formed a loosely knit freedom-fighting group known as the **Brigands**, who proceeded to launch attacks against the British, levelling plantations and terrorizing the island. In 1795, the Brigands captured Pigeon Island and held it for several weeks, but they were no match for British guns and military organization. Their numbers reduced and supplies exhausted, the rebels conceded defeat in 1798, striking a deal for their lives which saw them returned to slave labour.

Throughout the Brigand wars, fighting continued between the British and French, and the combination of Brigand attacks and colonial skirmishes saw most of the island's towns and villages razed to the ground. Many of the Anglo–French battles centred around possession of **Fort Charlotte**, the island's largest stockade, strategically placed in the Morne Fortune hills above the port of latter-day Castries. In 1796, the British launched a ferocious assault on French forces ensconced at the fort. After two days of solid fighting on steep hills, the 27th Royal Inniskilling Fusiliers broke the French resolve and the fort fell to the British, an important victory that represented the beginning of the end for French control over St Lucia.

St Lucia as a British colony

In 1814, the **Treaty of Paris** brought Anglo–French conflicts in the Caribbean to a long-overdue conclusion, with France ceding St Lucia to the British. Once the island was firmly established as a **crown colony**, St Lucian economics mirrored the pattern of slave-holding islands throughout the Caribbean. A brief period of prosperity followed the cessation of war, but this lasted only until the **abolition of slavery** in 1834. Though freed Africans were contracted to the plantations as indentured workers for a further four years, St Lucia's estates soon ceased to be profitable and the economy crumbled.

Despite the economic problems, the nineteenth century did see the British attempt to assert their presence on an island still dominated by French culture, customs and language. English commercial law was introduced in 1827 and after being made a member of the British Windward Islands in 1838, St Lucia's seat of government moved to the crown colony of Barbados; four years later, English was officially established as the island's language. None of these changes did anything to improve the flagging economy, though, and economic prosperity didn't return until the 1860s, when the exceptional natural port at Castries helped to make St Lucia a primary **coal warehousing centre** where steamships called to refuel. East Indian workers were imported to shore up the depleted labour force and the economy boomed for the next seventy-odd years. By the 1930s and 1940s, cheaper and more easily transportable diesel fuels had rendered the coaling industry obsolete and St Lucia entered a period of economic decline once again. Financial disparity and discontent were swift to follow and St Lucians hastened to form the island's first **trade unions**, which became the foundations of the political parties that later agitated for more influence over the government of their island.

By the late 1950s, the question of independence from Britain was looming, and small island nations such as St Lucia saw federalism as the most advantageous way forward. In 1958, St Lucia joined other British colonies in the **West Indies Federation**, a political grouping formed with the aim of winning independence. However, with new developments in their bauxite and oil industries, key members Jamaica and Trinidad and Tobago soon felt they were economically stable enough to stand alone, and their withdrawal, combined with petty rivalries between the members, saw the Federation weakened and finally dissolved in 1962. Despite the collapse of federalism, St Lucia was firmly on the road to independence, having been granted universal adult suffrage in 1951 and a new constitution in 1960. The constitution established an internal legislature in St Lucia, and the island's first political parties were quickly formed; by the time St Lucia was granted full self-government in 1967, a two-party system had developed, with the conservative, business-friendly United Workers Party (UWP) consolidating support and vying for power with the more liberal St Lucia Labour Party (SLP).

Independence

After years of lobbying, Britain finally acceded to the successive autonomy movements throughout the Caribbean and granted the new State of St Lucia **independence** on February 22, 1979; however, the island remains a Commonwealth country and a constitutional monarchy, with the British sovereign as the titular head of state, represented on the island by a governor general. Independence negotiations were fronted by the UWP under **John Compton**, a labour organizer who later became the main player of modern St Lucian politics. Despite Compton's central role, though, the party elected immediately after independence was the somewhat radical SLP. The Labour party was seen as the more progressive option, and the SLP's support for Communist Cuba and Maurice Bishop's revolutionary government of Grenada matched the popular anti-Imperialist sentiment of the time. However, voters were still loyal to Compton, and the UWP gained a strong majority in the 1982 election and retained its post in both the 1987 and 1992 ballots. A period of economic stability ensued, with the new tourism industry flourishing and continuing to boost foreign exchange, but the UWP and its leader lost favour after 1995, when hurricanes resulted in decreased banana production, strikes and rifts within the UWP. Compton resigned as prime minister in 1996, but retained a cabinet seat, and was succeeded by Dr Vaughan Lewis, a former director-general of the Organization of Eastern Caribbean States. Weakened by the absence of Compton, the faltering UWP lost decisively in the general election of

May 1997, when the SLP under Dr Kenny Anthony won all but one of the seventeen seats.

St Lucia today

Though relatively stable, the St Lucian **economy** has never been one of the region's strongest and today the island's number one foreign exchange earner is **tourism**, which contributes twelve percent of the GDP and employs one in three St Lucians of working age. **Agriculture** is the second-largest industry and more than a third of the island's population (some 60,000 people) are involved in the cultivation of **bananas**, which earns forty percent of St Lucia's export dollars. As in most Caribbean islands, bananas are grown by small family operations who market their crop through co-operatives such as the St Lucia Banana Corporation.

In the past, bananas were St Lucia's primary source of income, but recent **trade disputes** look set to have a devastating effect upon the St Lucian industry and the economic health of the island as a whole – all this in a country where a quarter of the population now lives below the poverty line. Disease and weighty production costs make it roughly three times more expensive to harvest Caribbean bananas than those grown in Latin America by more efficient US-based companies such as Chiquita, Dole and Del Monte. The main market for Caribbean bananas is the European Union (EU) and, since the early 1990s, **special trading privileges** have been awarded to some seventy developing nations, mostly former British and French colonies in the African, Caribbean and Pacific (ACP) union; the EU also imposed quotas and tariffs on Latin American producers and granted advantageous importation terms to European companies such as Geest and Fyffes, which market bananas in Europe via regional collectives.

ST LUCIA TODAY

The website of the Caribbean Banana
Exporters Association (Ⓦwww.cbea.org) carries an
up-to-date discussion of the current trade disputes.

Asserting that they had lost half of their UK sales, US-based banana producers responded to this in 1995 by **filing complaints** with the World Trade Organization, and a 1998 ruling agreed that the EU licensing and quota systems were discriminatory and did violate certain WTO laws. The EU responded by dispensing with individual country quotas and some import incentives, whilst still favouring ACP nations by guaranteeing a share of the market to the Caribbean. Still unsatisfied, the US and its partners refiled motions in 1999 with the WTO. In April 2001, the EU and USA reached an **agreement** on a new EU banana import regime, which came into operation on July 1, 2001. This agreement brought to an end more than eight years of disputes between the EU and the US, Ecuador and other Latin American states, but it has reduced the quota of Caribbean bananas that the US and the EU must take, favouring the cheaper and inferior Latin American bananas. Though there have been efforts to diversify into alternative crops such as peppers, mangoes and coconuts, these are far less valuable than "green gold", and the removal of the EU regime could well spell disaster for St Lucia and her neighbours.

St Lucia's economic **future** will now depend on finding alternative sources of income, including further tourist development, although – despite a boom in the industry in the 1990s – even this has been thinning out of late, as both tourism operators and the government try to reassess goals in the realization that quality and not quantity is essential in the Caribbean tourist market. Recently eco-tourism has come into play on the island, as locals have a greater awareness of

ST LUCIA TODAY

the importance of preserving St Lucia's natural resources: revenues are regularly channelled back into the upkeep, management and promotion of sites of ecological or historical interest such as rainforest trails (see pp.139–148) and the Heritage Tourism Program (see p.137). In comparison to other "tourist playgrounds" in the Caribbean, St Lucia has measured the industry's development, limiting the number of fenced-off all-inclusives and insisting that visitors are not corralled off into resort enclaves. At heart, the island and its culture remain relatively unaffected by the more negative consequences of tourism, even if some of the larger, more ostentatious hotels and resorts around Rodney Bay might lead the casual observer to think otherwise.

ST LUCIA TODAY

Culture and language

I n typical Caribbean fashion, the heart and soul of St Lucian culture is a syncretic amalgamation of the customs, languages, religions and societal norms of the island's French and British colonizers, and of the Africans that they brought with them.

Today's population of 158,000 is of predominantly African origin and some ninety percent of St Lucians are Roman Catholic, with the remainder divided between Protestant and Anglican faiths. However, though Christian hymns are sung lustily enough to raise the church roofs each Sunday, St Lucia is also a society in which esoteric African traditions of **magic and spiritualism** survive. Carnival is the best example of this fusion of Christianity and ancient belief: one of the stock characters of costume parades is the *moko jumbie*, a wildly attired figure on stilts representing the spirit world.

A secretive, mystical practice that also has its roots in African ancestor worship, **obeah** is woven into the fabric of local life, despite the fact that it's ostensibly illegal. Not everyone in St Lucia practices *obeah*, or even condones it,

236

but the more superstitious still call upon the obeahman –
gade in St Lucian Creole – to fix bad business partnerships
and love gone awry, or to attempt the removal of *jumbies*
(*zobis* in Creole), bad-tempered spirits that vex the life of
the common man. The obeahman does his work through
ritualistic use of herbs, rums, tobacco, potions and archaic
incantations, but as anti-*obeah* laws are still occasionally
enforced, casual visitors are unlikely to come into contact
with what remains an arcane practice.

Language is another aspect of St Lucian culture which
shows African influence. Though African languages were
suppressed as soon as slaves arrived on the island, French
planters still needed to communicate with their workers
and, gradually, the common language of **St Lucian Creole**
(*Kweyol*) – often called Patois – evolved, heavily laced with
French as well as African and English grammar and vocabulary. Though St Lucia's official language is **English**, *Kweyol*
is also spoken throughout the island, though it has only
recently appeared in written form. Spellings, punctuation
and word accents vary wildly as a result, and Patois remains
most efficient, not to mention melodious, when spoken:
several local radio and television programmes are conducted
entirely in *Kweyol* and the Folk Research Centre in Castries
is now home to the first Bible to be translated into St
Lucian Creole. The structure and pronunciation rely heavily on French: the word for dinner is "*dine*" (pronounced
dee-NAY), while St Lucia becomes *Set Lisi*, a plantain is a
"*banan*", sick is "*malad*" and please is "*su ple*". Mary W.
Toynbee's *A Visitor's Guide to St Lucian Patois* (see p.139) is
an excellent reference guide to the lingua franca.

Books

Where two publishers are given for the books listed below, they refer to the UK and US publisher respectively. Books published in one country only are followed by UK, US or St Lucia.

On the island, you might find books with St Lucian themes at the Sunshine Bookshop in the Point Seraphine shopping complex in Castries (see p.66).

Literature, poetry and memoir

Raija Nieminen *Voyage to the Island* (Gallaudet University Press, US). The autobiography of a deaf woman who moves to St Lucia with her husband from Finland and her discovery of a culture – and a kindness – different to anything she has known before.

Bob Shacochis *Easy in the Islands* (Picador; Penguin). A collection of short stories that centres on life in the islands and won the American Book Award.

Derek Walcott *Collected Poems 1948–1984, Omeros, The Bounty* (Faber & Faber, UK; Noonday Press, US; Ferrar, Strauss & Giroux, UK/US). A poem of exile and spiritual travel in the West Indies that utilizes the framework of Homer's *Iliad* and *Odyssey*, the cadence of the epic *Omeros* is purely West Indian while *The Bounty* is a collection of poems inspired by the arrival of the British ship in

1787 on St Lucian shores. *Collected Poems* provides a good overview of the Nobel Prize-winner's early work.

Herman Wouk *Don't Stop the Carnival* (Harper Collins; Little, Brown & Co). Lively, humorous, but slightly dated tale of a Broadway publicity agent who buys a small inn on a Caribbean island.

History, culture and language

Lawrence Carrington *Dictionary of St Lucian Creole* (Mouton De Gruyter, US). A rich and fascinating dictionary of the native language.

Robert J. Devaux *Pigeon Island National Landmark: A Brief History and Guide* (St Lucia National Trust, St Lucia). Colour pamphlet with the history of the island from Arawak to modern times.

J.P. Parry, Philip Sherlock & Anthony Maingot *A Short History of the West Indies* (Caribbean Publishing, UK). The best concise history of the region, taking the story up to

the mid-1980s and good on general issues like regional cooperation and debt crisis.

Polly Pattullo *Last Resorts – The Cost of Tourism in the Caribbean* (Cassell; Monthly Review Press). Important and well-researched critique of the tourist industry and its impact on the islands, with many references to St Lucia.

Mary W. Toynbee *A Visitor's Guide to St Lucian Patois* (Lithographic Press, St Lucia). An easy-to-read reference guide, written in a light tone, with a dictionary, common phrases and short history of Patois etymology.

Specialist guides

Peter Evans *Birds of the Eastern Caribbean* (Caribbean Publishing, UK). Lists nearly three hundred birds native to the Eastern Caribbean, with colour photos and charts to locate by island.

Colleen Ryan *The Complete Diving Guide: The Caribbean (Vol. 1)* (Complete Dive Guide Publications; Cruising Guide

Publications). Write-ups of dive sites and operators and other such useful information interlaced with tales of personal experience and lots of interesting trivia.

INDEX

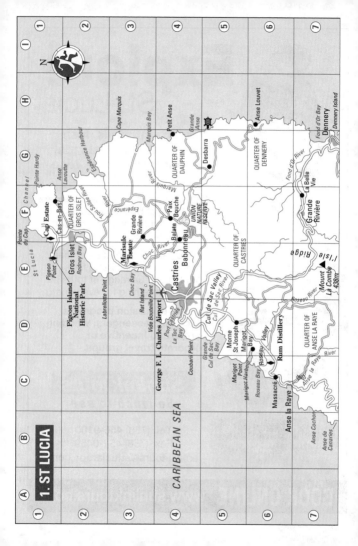

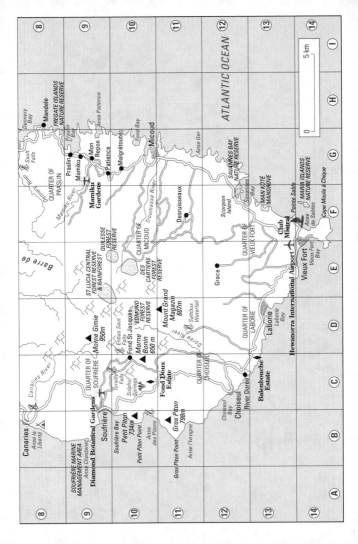

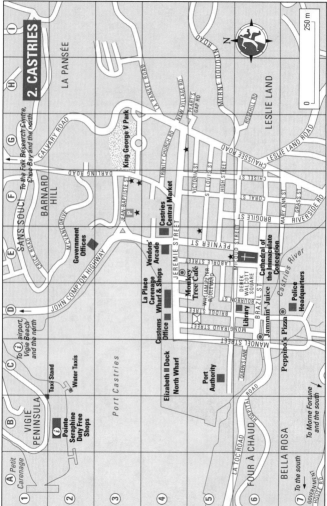

2. CASTRIES

VIGIE PENINSULA

A Petit Carenage

Pointe Seraphine Duty Free Shops

To ① airport, Vigie Beach and the north

Taxi Stand

Water Taxis

Port Castries

Elizabeth II Dock
North Wharf

Customs Office

La Place Carenage Wharf & Shops

Port Authority

LA TOC ROAD

CAP ESTATE ROAD

QUEENS LANE

FOUR À CHAUD

BELLA ROSA

To Morne Fortune and the south

To the south

GOVERNMENT HOUSE RD

Peppino's Pizza

Police Headquarters

Jammin Juice

Library

Derek Walcott Square

Brazil St

Bourbon St

Mongraud Street

Manael Street

Chausee Road

Bridge Street

Micoud Street

Laborie Street

Wm. Peter Boulevard

Jeremie St

Monkey Tree Café

Peynier Street

Government Offices

McLane Drive

John Compton Highway

BARNARD HILL

SANS SOUCI

To the Folk Research Centre, Choc Bay and the north

Calvary Road

Chisel Road

Darling Road

Jean-Baptiste St

Vendors' Arcade

Castries Central Market

King George V Park

LA PANSÉE

La Pansée Road

New Village Rd

Peat's Gap Rd

Rosehill Rd

Morne Dudon Road

Trinity Church Rd

Victoria St

S. Louis St

High Street

Coral St

Chisel St

Mary Ann St

Grass St

Riverside Rd

Brogile St

Castries River

Cathedral of the Immaculate Conception

LESLIE LAND

Leslie Land Road

Chaussee Road

N

0   250 m

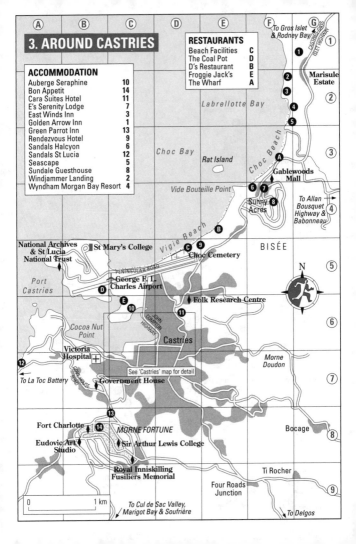

3. AROUND CASTRIES

ACCOMMODATION

Auberge Seraphine	10
Bon Appetit	14
Cara Suites Hotel	11
E's Serenity Lodge	7
East Winds Inn	3
Golden Arrow Inn	1
Green Parrot Inn	13
Rendezvous Hotel	9
Sandals Halcyon	6
Sandals St Lucia	12
Seascape	5
Sundale Guesthouse	8
Windjammer Landing	2
Wyndham Morgan Bay Resort	4

RESTAURANTS

Beach Facilities	C
The Coal Pot	D
D's Restaurant	B
Froggie Jack's	E
The Wharf	A

To Gros Islet & Rodney Bay

Marisule Estate

Labrellotte Bay

Choc Bay

Rat Island

Choc Beach

Gablewoods Mall

To Allan Bousquet Highway & Babonneau

Sunny Acres

Vide Bouteille Point

Vigie Beach

BISÉE

National Archives & St Lucia National Trust

St Mary's College

Choc Cemetery

Port Castries

PENINSULAR ROAD

George F.L. Charles Airport

Folk Research Centre

JOHN COMPTON HIGHWAY

Castries

Cocoa Nut Point

Victoria Hospital

Morne Doudon

See 'Castries' map for detail

GRASS STREET

Government House

To La Toc Battery

Fort Charlotte

MORNE FORTUNE

Bocage

Eudovic Art Studio

Sir Arthur Lewis College

Royal Inniskilling Fusiliers Memorial

Ti Rocher

Four Roads Junction

To Cul de Sac Valley, Marigot Bay & Soufrière

To Delgos

0   1 km

N

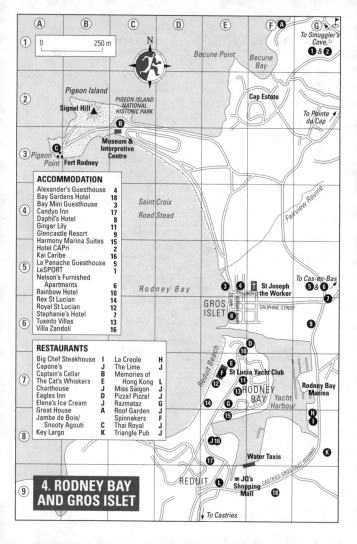

ACCOMMODATION

Alexander's Guesthouse	4
Bay Gardens Hotel	18
Bay Mini Guesthouse	3
Candyo Inn	17
Daphil's Hotel	8
Ginger Lily	11
Glencastle Resort	9
Harmony Marina Suites	15
Hotel CAPri	2
Kai Caribe	16
La Panache Guesthouse	5
LeSPORT	1
Nelson's Furnished Apartments	6
Rainbow Hotel	10
Rex St Lucian	14
Royal St Lucian	12
Stephanie's Hotel	7
Tuxedo Villas	13
Villa Zandoli	16

RESTAURANTS

Big Chef Steakhouse	I	La Creole	H
Capone's	J	The Lime	J
Captain's Cellar	B	Memories of	
The Cat's Whiskers	E	Hong Kong	L
Charthouse	J	Miss Saigon	J
Eagles Inn	D	Pizza! Pizza!	J
Elena's Ice Cream	J	Razmataz	G
Great House	A	Roof Garden	J
Jambe de Bois/		Spinnakers	F
Snooty Agouti	C	Thai Royal	J
Key Largo	K	Triangle Pub	J

4. RODNEY BAY AND GROS ISLET

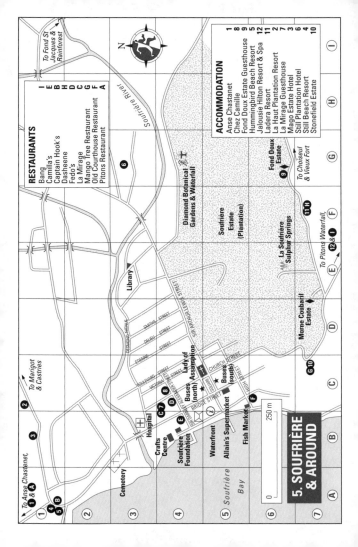

5. SOUFRIÈRE & AROUND

RESTAURANTS

Bang	I
Camilla's	E
Captain Hook's	B
Dasheene	H
Fedo's	D
La Mirage	C
Mango Tree Restaurant	G
Old Courthouse Restaurant	F
Pitons Restaurant	A

ACCOMMODATION

Anse Chastanet	1
Chez Camille	8
Fond Doux Estate Guesthouse	9
Hummingbird Beach Resort	5
Jalousie Hilton Resort & Spa	12
Ladera Resort	11
La Haut Plantation Resort	2
La Mirage Guesthouse	7
Mago Estate Hotel	3
Still Plantation Hotel	6
Still Beach Resort	4
Stonefield Estate	10

To Fond St Jacques & Rainforest

To Marigot & Castries

To Anse Chastenet

To Choiseul & Vieux Fort

To Pitons Waterfall

Soufrière River

Diamond Botanical Gardens & Waterfall

Soufrière Estate (Plantation)

Library

La Soufrière Sulphur Springs

Fond Doux Estate

Morne Coubaril Estate

SMITHS STREET
CAZELI STREET
CEMETERY AVENUE
SIR ARTHUR LEWIS STREET

PALMISTE STREET
VICTORIA STREET
MAURICE MASON STREET
CHURCH STREET
BRIDGE STREET
HIGH STREET

Hospital

Crafts Centre

Soufrière Foundation

Waterfront

Allain's Supermarket

Fish Market

Lady of Assumption

Buses (north)

Buses (south)

Cemetery

Soufrière Bay

250 m

0